YouTube Affiliate Marketing Secrets for 2019:

Growth Hacking & Digital Marketing Strategies to Make Money Online With YouTube Affiliate Marketing; Build a Profitable Passive Income Business With Step-by-Step Social Media Video Marketing Guide

Content

Introduction 4

How to Research Your Physical Product?................................6

Criteria Five 7

Creating Your Video Review 17

The Exact Method..18

Video Optimization 23

Google & YouTube Optimization...32

How to Look for Problems in Any Niche?......................................36

How Do I Get my Affiliate Product? 48

Product Review 53

Upload & Optimize the Video...62

Boost the SEO Rankings 66

What to Know about Earning Money with Videos................................69

Creating Engaging Video Content on YouTube 72

How to get More YouTube Subscribers 78

Selling on YouTube with Affiliate Marketing.................................90

Using AdSense on YouTube 99

A Profitable YouTube Business Model 105

What it Takes to be Successful at YouTube 110

How to Monetize your Videos the right way 116

Integrating YouTube Marketing 123

How to Build a Successful YouTube Channel 125

Tips for a Successful YouTube Channel..............................130

More tricks for Earning and Creating Traffic......................139

YouTube Audience Growth Secrets 2019 145

Conclusion..160

Introduction

If you're looking for a new source of income but you don't have huge capital to get started, then this business model is for you.

The great thing about this idea is it's not rocket science. You don't need any complicated skills to make money.

If you can count from 1 to 100, then you can make money through Amazon affiliate marketing.

The process is also very doable.

1 – Find a Product

2 – Create a video review

3 – Optimize and upload the video on YouTube

4 – Rank the video on Google and YouTube

If you can follow these 4 steps, then you'll be making a new source of income in no time.

Now, am I guaranteeing that you'll make X amount of money.

NO.

I don't know you, your work ethic and your motivations.

But what I do know is you picked up this book because you want a side-hustle.

You want to make money on the side.

And that what I'm going to help you do.

How to Research Your Physical Product?

If you're old enough to remember road-tripping (or going to a designated place) without Google Maps or Waze, then you know how painful it is to find the exact location of the place you're going to.

It's hard to find something when you don't know what you're looking for. You need a map for a road-trip and you need a map for a treasure hunt.

They are the guide for me to choose the best product possible with the best chances of making money through YouTube reviews.

Is it perfect? No.

It cannot guarantee profitability.

But it does increase your chances of NOT wasting anytime selling products that will most probably not going to sell.

Follow these criteria and aim to get 4 out of 5.

Criteria Five

Criteria #1 – Price is $50 and above

I want to promote $50+ products because Amazon only gives around 3%-10% in affiliate commissions. So for cheap products, we're not really gonna earn big commissions. However, if the quantity of the market is good, I would still sell cheap products just to get click to my Amazon affiliate link. (later you'll know why and how a cheap product can still make you hundreds of dollars in affiliate commissions - almost accidentally)

Criteria #2 – YouTube Competition is Existent

There should be other people already reviewing the product.

I prefer to sell and review product at 500-10,000 search results when you search for the product on YouTube.

nerf mega lightning bow	Q

Filters ▾   About 8,260 results

For first time Amazon associates, I suggest that you focus on 500-3,000 searches for the product name/for "nerf mega lightning bow review" keyword.

Criteria #3 – At Least 50-150 Reviews (80% 5 stars)

The product must have at least 50-150 reviews on Amazon. This is, I believe, the sweet spot for non-competitive but still profitable products.

Choose 300++ Amazon reviewed products and you'll be in competition with long-time Amazon associates.

Criteria #4 – There Are Cheaper Substitutes or Complementary Products

There should be other products available highly related to the one you're promoting.

Always choose at least 3 more products that you can promote outside the main-product.

Criteria #5 – You or Someone You Know Already Have the Product

Although you can review a product without having it on hand, it's still better to review something that you or someone you know already uses the product.

EXAMPLE RESEARCH:

Here's an example research and evaluation for a product.

First, I'll go to Amazon and look for different categories.

There's lot of great departments in here like:

Home, Garden & Tools

Home

Kitchen & Dining

Furniture

Bedding & Bath

Appliances

Patio, Lawn & Garden

Fine Art

Arts, Crafts & Sewing

Pet Supplies

Beauty & Health

All Beauty

Luxury Beauty

Professional Skin Care

Salon & Spa

Sports & Outdoors

Athletic Clothing

Exercise & Fitness

Hunting & Fishing

Team Sports

Fan Shop

These are 3 of my favorites.

So let's say I chose Camping & Hiking as my category.

What I'll do is spend 10-20 minutes just browsing around the product line.

While browsing, I keep the criteria in mind and find something that may match that criteria.

Once I found something interesting, I will run it through the criteria.

lifestraw mission gravity water purifier

Filters ▾

I tried with the keyword" water purifier system"

Criteria #1 – Price is $50 and above

List Price: ~~$154.95~~
Price: $116.98 + $84.1?
You Save: $37.97 (25%)

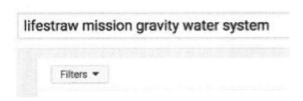
lifestraw mission gravity water system

Filters ▾

Criteria #2 – YouTube Competition is Existent

Only 500-1k searches.

For the keyword "lifestraw mission gravity water system"

There are also a handful of others reviewing or testing the product:

LifeStraw Mission test
Outsite.org
2 years ago · 8,573 views
Lifestraw Mission er et nyt vandfilter der har en vandpose på 5 eller 12 liter og kan rense 18000 liter vand, eller nok til en person i ...
CC

Lifestraw Mission quick look
The Rambler
5 months ago · 58 views
A quick overview of the Lifestraw Mission water purifier. See the full review at ...

Lifestraw Mission
Papica Bushcraft
1 year ago · 4,871 views
www.tuleloviz.hu.

Criteria #3 – At Least 50-150 Reviews (80% 5 stars)

LifeStraw

LifeStraw Mission Water Purification System, High-Volume Gravity-Fed Purifier for Camping and Emergency Preparedness

★★★★☆ ▾　101 customer reviews | 38 answered questions

Criteria #4 – There Are Cheaper Substitutes or Complementary Products

Criteria #5 – You or Someone You Know Already Have the Product

I do have some friends who has similar products but I'm not sure if they have this exact brand. So I'm giving this an X for now.

We still got 4 out of 5 so I'll still consider reviewing this product.

I'm a camping enthusiast myself so this is something that I would also consider buying.

Once you got a product that you want to promote, just go to Amazon's associate page and register for a free account.

https://affiliate-program.amazon.com/

Inside your account, you can search for your product name or the ASIN to get your affiliate link.

Before we can pay you, we must have your Payment Method information and Tax Information. information.

Welcome to Associates Central

Quickly Add Links

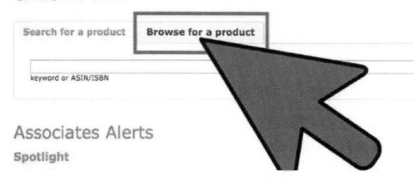

Search for a product | **Browse for a product**

keyword or ASIN/ISBN

Associates Alerts

Spotlight

Customize and Get HTML

Build a link to a specific page from Amazon using the tools below.

Signed in as spesgoa-20 ▾ Tracking ID spesgoa-20 ▾

Text and Image | Text Only | **Image Only**

1. Customize Link	2. Preview
	To create this link, cut and paste the HTML code in the lower left textbox into your web page.
Link Text: A1 Kraton Handle Plain Zytel Sheath	A1 Kraton Handle Plain Zytel Sheath

3. Get HTML Code For This Product Link

Highlight and copy the HTML below, then paste it into the code for your Web site.

```
<a href="http://www.amazon.com/gp/product/B001D2H482
/ref=as_li_as_tl?ie=UTF8&camp=1789&creative=390957&
creativeASIN=B001D2H482&linkCode=as2&tag=spesgoa-20">A1
Kraton Handle Plain Zytel Sheath</a><img
src="http://www.assoc-amazon.com/e/ir?t=spesgoa-20&l=as2&
o=1&a=B001D2H482" width="1" height="1" border="0" alt=""
```

[Highlight HTML]

Note: Your Associates ID, **spesgoa-20**, is already embedded in the code.

Save it for now and move to the next step.

Creating Your Video Review

You don't need any fancy camera or tools to create your video review.

Just use your smartphone and install some video editing software on your computer. There's lots of free stuff out there, do I need to teach you how to search on Google? Hopefully not.

Your review should be at least 5-7 minutes.

That's the time-frame that I found to be the best when it comes to product reviews.

I have my own step by step process for doing a product review and you can choose to follow it at first before you tweak it and create your own.

There's no one magic formula that will work for all of your reviews.

Each product has their own unique features and benefits that it's almost impossible to only have one step by step formula to follow for all your reviews.

So try my method and then keep improving it based on what your product is.

The Exact Method

Step 1 – What Is It?

The first step is to show the product and mention what is it. Then tell them what they should expect from this video.

Step 2 – What Problem Does It Solve?

The next step is to mention exactly what the product is.

What problem does it solve?

Does it eliminate dandruff?

Does it increase my Archery range?

Whatever it is, give the biggest benefit and the main use in 2-3 sentences.

Step 3 – Demo

This is not always possible, but if you can, try to give a demonstration of the product.

If they can see the product while you're using it, then they will see themselves more in your position (using the product) and that'll make them more likely to buy the product.

Step 4 – Amazon Reviews

Next, mention some reviews from other people. You can read snippets of Amazon reviews and just give them an idea of what other people think.

Try to find somethings that people say over and over again about the product. These are mostly the most important things that customers care about.

Also, by reading some Amazon reviews you'll be able to gather social proof. You're not just the one recommending the product to strangers. You also have other people vouch for the product.

That's powerful stuff!

Step 5 – Pros and Cons

You can find most pros and cons on the Amazon review itself.

Read the 5 star ones and lower star reviews.

By reading these reviews, you'll know exactly what people want and what people didn't like about the product.

Mention at least 4 pros for every 1 con.

Step 6 – Substitutes and Complementary Products

This part builds up to what you did in step 5.

If you read the negative reviews, you'll know exactly what they didn't like about the product.

Maybe it's too expensive. Then promote something cheaper with almost the same quality.

Mention 3 different product that may compete (or complement) the product you're promoting.

Note: If you're promoting cheap products, it's better to put more products on your description. Put at least 3-5 substitute/complementary products so you'll get more chances of getting clicks. The thing about these clicks is they don't necessarily have to buy the exact cheap product for you to make money.

Amazon has "cookies" that tracks the clicker and everything they buy on Amazon in the next 48 hours (after they click your affiliate link) will be credited to you.

So it means if they happen to buy a large screen $2,000 TV, you'll get the commissions for that purchase. There's no guarantee that they will buy anything but it still a great way to make extra income.

This is why you shouldn't necessarily step away from cheaper products. If the market is big enough, you'll get enough clicks and probably even some "accidental" purchases.

Step 7 – Call to Action

The last step is to ask them to buy the product.

Don't be afraid to ask for the sale.

Let them know that it's a really great product and make them click your link. Also, be honest with your agenda. Tell them that you're gonna make a commission if they buy through your Amazon associate link.

Video Optimization

Before you upload your video, I want to teach you how to find your keywords first.

Generally, your main keyword will be your product name or product name + "review".

Now, we don't just want to rank our video with this keyword. We also want people to find us through other related ones.

Keyword Research

So go to Google Keyword Planner and search for your product.

https://adwords.google.com/home/tools/keyword-planner/

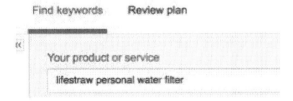

Then arrange the monthly searches and competition from low to high.

Look for at least 5 keywords that has 100-1k monthly searches.

| how does the lifestraw work | 100 – 1K | Low |

Find something that indicated that they are looking for a product like the one you're promoting.

Keyword (by relevance)	searches ?	?
lifestraw review	1K – 10K	Medium
mec lifestraw	10 – 100	Medium
lifestraw home	10 – 100	Medium
vestergaard lifestraw	100 – 1K	Medium
clean sip water filter straw	10 – 100	Medium
price of lifestraw	10 – 100	Medium

The higher the BUYER INTENT is, the better.

For example, someone who searches for:

Buy Water Purifier for Camping

is more likely to buy than the one who searches for:

How to Use a Water Purifier

But this one above still has a higher buyer intent than:

Water purifier

You can find Buyer Intent keywords by looking at keywords like:

Buy

How to use

Where to buy

Ways to

Price of

Get at least 5 keywords and save em'

* * * *

Uploading & Optimization

Now it's time to upload your video.

(*you can upload your video here*:

https://www.youtube.com/upload)

Follow these optimization tactics to help you get ranked faster and get more views:

#1 – The File Name

Always change your file name to whatever your product name is.

Don't use random file names like video2342.mp4

Change it to "productname.mp4" instead.

This helps in making YouTube know that your video is all about that product.

#2 – The Title

The next one is the title.

Don't just use your main keyword.

Add some of the keywords you got and combine them with the main keyword.

E.g.

Lifestraw Water Purifier Review| Comparing Different Water Purifiers

Lifestraw Shake Bottle| Prices of Lifestraw and Are They Legit?

Adding extra keyword will let you:

- Add other keyword/s and make them rank on Google and YouTube too

- Increase the click through rate by having a more "clickbait'ish" type of title. It's better than having "product name review" as your title.

#3 – The Description

I make the description short and simple.

I put the main product and the affiliate link.

```
Lifestraw Water Purifier System Review
http://amazonassociatelink.com/producta

How to use a water purifier
where to buy water purifier
buying lifestraw water purifier system
lifestraw scam
is lifestraw legit

product b
http://amazonassociatelink.com/productb

product c
http://amazonassociatelink.com/productc
```

Then I add the 5 keywords I researches a while ago.

Next, I'll also add the product names and affiliate links of the substitute products (if there's any).

Tags (e.g., albert einstein, flying pig, mashup)

#4 – The Tags

I'll put the keywords on the tag section and I'll even add some more less competitive keywords on it.

#5 – The Thumbnail

Personally, the best thumbnails for Amazon product reviews are just you with the product (or just the product) and add some text on it.

E.g.

MacBook (2017) Review | TechRanger.net
TechRanger.Net
1 month ago • 27,867 views
Our review of the new 2017 Apple MacBook 12 inch. Only in it's third
iteration, the MacBook is one of the defining laptops of the ...
4K   CC

iPod Touch 6th Generation Review - 2015 iPod Touch 6G

EverythingApplePro 🅴🆁
2 years ago · 1,464,628 views
All New Apple iPod Touch 6th Generation Review. Ultimate iPod Touch 6th Gen Detailed Review. 6G Camera, Speed Test, Puppy ...

Modern Slickback (Suavecito Pomade Review) | Men's Hairstyle Tutorial

Cavin Vanderpoel
2 years ago · 187,289 views
Don't forget to subscribe! → http://bit.ly/HighveldStyle I say "um" a lot in this video! ···································...

Suavecito Pomade Review | Men's Hair Product Review

Alaenio
4 months ago · 2,139 views
Check out this Suavecito Pomade Review. This particular one is the Firme Holde version. This is one of my favorite Men's ...

#6 – The Playlist

Add the product's category on your playlist.

Google & YouTube Optimization

This one will be a breeze to implement.

Go to http://Konker.io and look for the SEO category.

Hire at least 2 different freelancers with from 2 different categories.

All in SEO

Backlinks

Social Signals

Content Creation

PBN Links

Expired Domains

PBN Creation

Keyword Research

Youtube SEO

Site Creation

Buy Domains

Site Optimization

I recommend PBN LINKS & SOCIAL SIGNALS.

Only choose someone who has 100+ 5 star reviews:

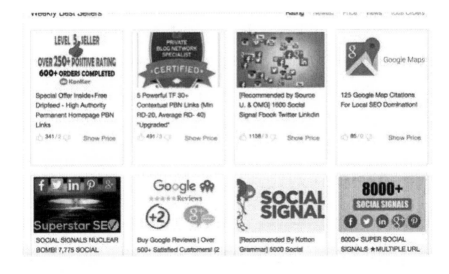

Also, don't spend more than $30 for one service.

Read the reviews and look for "specific" and "result based" testimonials. It's better to find something like "my keyword ranked on 1st page in less than 3 days" rather than "I like the service".

You want results – that's it.

You can get results in 1-3 weeks' time.

If your keywords are super competitive, then you have to wait a little bit more time and maybe even add some more backlinks to it.

Conclusion

You can now start your own side-hustle business.

I don't think that you need more than 1-2 hours per day to implement this business idea.

So set aside some time every day and keep working on your skills.

You can't just choose any product and expect it to make money on the first day.

Sometimes, it requires trial and error on your part.

Nothing is guaranteed.

But one thing I'm sure of is you won't make any money if you never get started in the first place.

So take that first step today.

Do something, do the little things that will eventually lead you to making a full-time income online.

Good luck!

How to Look for Problems in Any Niche?

Before you find a product, it'll be better to find a problem first.

Remember, all products are answers to a problem.

And problems can be mined from different sources.

#1 – Google Search

You can always start with Google.

Just by searching for "problem", you'll be able to identify a market that you can target.

E.g.

Top disease killers in America

Top disease killers in America

All　News　Images　Videos　More　　　　Settings　Tools

About 2,660,000 results (0.69 seconds)

The top 10 leading causes of death in the U.S.:

- Heart disease.
- Cancer (malignant neoplasms)
- Chronic lower respiratory disease.
- Accidents (unintentional injuries)
- Stroke (cerebrovascular diseases)
- Alzheimer's disease.
- Diabetes.
- Influenza and pneumonia.

More items...

The top 10 leading causes of death in the United States
www.medicalnewstoday.com/articles/282929.php

All   Images   News   Videos   More   Settings   Tools

About 2,120,000 results (0.61 seconds)

The top 10 leading causes of death in the U.S.:

- Heart disease.
- Cancer (malignant neoplasms)
- Chronic lower respiratory disease.
- Accidents (unintentional injuries)
- Stroke (cerebrovascular diseases)
- Alzheimer's disease.
- Diabetes.
- Influenza and pneumonia.

    More items...

The top 10 leading causes of death in the United States
www.medicalnewstoday.com/articles/282929.php

most common infections in us

So, without further ado, here are the five most common infectious diseases.

- Hepatitis-B. According to current statistics, hepatitis-B is the most common infectious disease in the world, affecting some 2 billion people -- that's more than one-quarter of the world's population. ...
- Malaria. ...
- Hepatitis-C. ...
- Dengue. ...
- Tuberculosis.

The 5 Most Common Infectious Diseases -- The Motley Fool
https://www.fool.com/investing/general/.../the-5-most-common-infectious-diseases.aspx

About this result   Fee

Also, you don't need to target super serious problems.

You can target everyday problems or at least, less serious ones (not deadly ones).

common problems of millenials

5 Shocking Statistics About Real Millennial Problems - All Groan Up
allgroanup.com › TWENTYSOMETHING LIFE ▾
Millennial Problems #1: Millennials are the largest generation at over 85-90 ... is currently the second most common cause of death among college students.".

Biggest problems in world today, according to millennials ...
www.businessinsider.com/world-economic-forum-world-biggest-problems-concernin... ▾
Aug 23, 2016 - The 10 most critical problems in the world, according to millennials. ... In one survey, WEF asked respondents to name the three most serious issues affecting the world today. ... Below are the top-10 most concerning world issues, according to millennials.

What are the most common issues that millennials face today? How do ...
https://www.quora.com/What-are-the-most-common-issues-that-millennials-face-toda... ▾
Thanks for the A2A. Issue: The predetermined constraints of our western society that all people, including millenials, are expected to conform to. This one is going to ...

3 Major Challenges Facing Millennials – RELEVANT Magazine
https://relevantmagazine.com/life/3-major-challenges-facing-millennials ▾
Aug 5, 2015 - Yet, the millennial generation is experiencing real challenges. ... Many want to blame millennials' problems on the fact that we're entitled and ...

#2 – Your Own Problem

You can also look and search for your own problems.

What is bothering you right now?

What are the things that you want to change for yourself?

E.g.

Right now, I wanna lose my belly fat or my dad bod.

All   Images   Videos   News   More   Settings   Tools

About 530,000 results (0.54 seconds)

6 Weight Loss Tips to Combat the Dad Bod | Eat This Not That
www.eatthis.com/6-ways-combat-dad-bod ▾
At first, the viral sensation of "**Dad Bod**" looks like the best thing to happen to men since the launch of ESPN. Six-pack abs and rapid weight **loss**. are out—six ...

The Barry's Bootcamp Anti-'Dad Bod' Workout - Men's Fitness
www.mensfitness.com/training/workout.../high-intensity-anti-dad-bod-workout ▾
"My suggestion to Dads: do my workout and **lose** the 10 pounds. Do you really ... Do this 20-minute Anti- '**Dad Bod**' routine from DeGrazio three times a week.

How I Lost my Dad Bod in Just 12 Weeks - This Dad Does
thisdaddoes.com/lose-dad-bod-12-weeks/ ▾
Dec 14, 2015 - **Losing** my **Dad bod** was one of the biggest challenges of my life. It took me hours of discipline, exercises and hard work. The results speak for ...

---

ways to lose belly fat

All   Videos   Images   News   More   Settings   Tools

About 1,200,000 results (0.67 seconds)

20 Effective Tips to Lose Belly Fat (Backed by Science) - Healthline
www.healthline.com/nutrition/20-tips-to-lose-belly-fat ▾
Jul 11, 2016 - Many people store fat in the belly, and losing fat from this area can be hard. Here are 20 effective tips to lose belly fat, based on studies.
12 Things That Make You Gain ... · High-fiber foods · How Intermittent Fasting Can ...

6 Simple Ways to Lose Belly Fat, Based on Science - Healthline
www.healthline.com/nutrition/6-proven-ways-to-lose-belly-fat ▾
Nov 30, 2016 - Belly fat is the most harmful fat in your body, linked to many diseases. Here are 6 simple ways to lose belly fat that are supported by science.
20 Effective Tips to Lose Belly ... · Fiber Can Help You Lose ... · Meat · Whey protein

9 Proven Ways To Lose Stubborn Belly Fat - Prevention
www.prevention.com/weight-loss/...loss-tips/new-research-on-how-to-lose-belly-fat ▾
Jul 18, 2014 - Belly fat is more than just a wardrobe malfunction. Learn how to lose belly fat and increase health from Prevention Magazine.

#3 – Someone Else's Problem

Don't just focus on yourself, this is where most of my "problem ideas" comes from.

I ask other people like my friends, family, co-workers, etc. about their problems.

If you're really concern about them and you tell them that you're looking for a solution, then they will share it with you.

Just be genuine and honest.

Remember, they are telling you something personal – so keep it personal and don't share it to others.

#4 – Google Keyword Planner

https://adwords.google.com/KeywordPlanner

Once you have some problems that needs solving, the next step is to find some keywords to target.

So basically, if someone is having problems with losing belly fat, you'll just search for it on the Keyword Planner and then arrange them by low monthly and searches and low to high competition.

Your product or service

| belly fat | Get Ideas |

This page shows ranges for search volumes. For a more detailed view, set up and run a campaign. |

I will get at least 5 keywords to target as part of my promotion.

So what keyword should you pick?

Well I recommend keywords that has 100-1000 monthly searches with LOW competition.

how to lose excess belly fat	100 – 1K	Low
ways to lose your stomach	100 – 1K	Low
how to lose a big belly	100 – 1K	Low

Ad group ideas Keyword ideas		
Keyword (by relevance)	Avg. monthly searches [?]	Competition [?]
how to drop belly fat	100 – 1K	Low
tips to reduce fat belly	10 – 100	Low
how to lose the fat around your s…	10 – 100	Low
how to lose fat from stomach fast	10 – 100	Low
losing stomach fat diet	10 – 100	Low
how to shed stomach fat	100 – 1K	Low

Save 5 of these on a notepad. You'll use this on the latter chapter.

The Problem Eradicator Research

If you still don't have any idea on what topic to target, then you can just use this method for finding keywords or topics to target.

What you'll do is search for keywords like:

Ways to

How to

Where to buy

Price of

Solve my

Eliminate my

Eliminate the

How to get rid of

Get rid of

These are keywords that indicates that they want to solve something or find out something. They are experiencing some kind of pain or desire to solve a specific problem.

E.g.

Ad group ideas	Keyword ideas		Columns
Keyword (by relevance)		**Avg. monthly searches ?**	**Competition ?**
to rid of		100 – 1K	Low
catch fruit flies with vinegar and ...		10 – 100	Low
rid of something		10 – 100	Low
fruit flies all over the house		10 – 100	Low
rid of them		10 – 100	Low
synonyms for getting rid of		100 – 1K	Low
get rid of me meaning		100 – 1K	Low
meaning of get rid of		100 – 1K	Low

solve the linear system using eli...	10 – 100	Low	--
equations by elimination	10 – 100	Low	--
linear systems elimination	100 – 1K	Low	...
solving linear equations elimination	10 – 100	Low	--
system by elimination	100 – 1K	Low	--
how to get rid of fruit flies with di...	10 – 100	Low	--
solve each system by elimination	1K – 10K	Low	$3.62

how to not stress	1K – 10K	Low	$1.84
elimination method math	100 – 1K	Low	$0.03
how do you solve a system of eq...	100 – 1K	Low	$2.29
how to stop procrastinating	10K – 100K	Low	$0.59

You will see a lot of search terms people are typing.

Follow the same rule when choosing a keyword.

A – 100-1,000 monthly searches

B – LOW competition

How Do I Get my Affiliate Product?

Once I got a problem that needs to get solved, I'll go to Clickbank's marketplace and start searching for solutions or problem.

https://accounts.clickbank.com/marketplace.htm

I'll just type my topic and look if there are products available to promote.

(signup here first: https://accounts.clickbank.com/signup/)

Back to the marketplace…

Before I choose any product, I'll run it first through my own 4 point criteria.

#1 – There Must Be a Sales Video

I like sales video because they are easier to use as call to action in the review. Also, they tend to convert generally higher than a sales letter.

#2 – Gravity of 30-100

This is the number of affiliates who made 1-2 sales in the past 4 weeks.

I aim for 30-100 because it means the product is selling and at the same time, there's an "okay" amount of competition. 100+ would not be ideal for a newbie.

#3 – Avg. Commission of $30

This is a personal choice. I like to make at least $30 per sale. For beginners, this is a perfect starting point.

But after your first few profitable project, you can start targeting more expensive products at the $100-$2,000 range.

#4 – There Are Other YouTube Reviews

There must be also other people doing a review of that product on YouTube.

It only means people are actually looking for it.

If the product reviews are getting an average of 300 views, then that's a good sign people are watching and looking for that product review.

So let's run these criteria through a product that I found.

#1 – There Must Be a Sales Video:

This one has one and it's a good one too.

#2 – Gravity of 30-100:

.0% | Grav: 134.49

It's 134 so it doesn't match the criteria.

I wouldn't recommend this as your first product review.

But for 3rd, 4th try… then it's a good one.

#3 – Avg. Commission of $30

Avg $/sale
$38.30

PROMOTE

Yep!

#4 – There Are Other YouTube Reviews

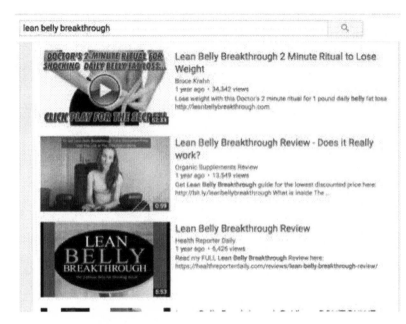

Product Review

For the product review itself, I recommend that you just use powerpoint or keynote to record your review.

Both of em' got a function that allows you to record audio and turn the presentation into a "screen recorded" video.

As you already know, there's tons of reviews on YouTube (duhh) and each one of em' has its own style. Just because one formula works for one niche doesn't mean it'll always work for the others.

So you have to test how you do your reviews.

In this chapter, I'll show you how I create mine.

This works for me and I'm hoping that it'll work for you too. Also, I'm going to give you a sample slide to copy so you'll know how I do mine.

Note: My reviews are usually just 5-7 minutes short.

STEP BY STEP PROCESS

Step 1 – What Will I Get?

The first step is to just tell them what they're going to learn in the video.

Give them a brief overview of what the product is all about. 1-2 sentences would be fine.

Step 2 – Benefits

The next step is to mention the benefits of the product.

When you're talking about the benefits of the product, remember to talk about them.

What will they gain?

What pain will they avoid?

What desires will they fulfill?

Answer these 3 questions and you got your powerful benefits.

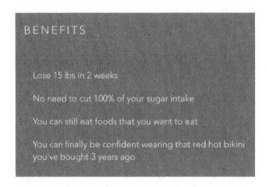

BENEFITS

Lose 15 lbs in 2 weeks

No need to cut 100% of your sugar intake

You can still eat foods that you want to eat

You can finally be confident wearing that red hot bikini you've bought 3 years ago

Step 3 – Features

The features are about the product.

If the benefits are "what will they gain?"

The features are "what will they get?"

These are the technical aspects of the product.

These are the e-book, manual, shipping time, access to a membership site, access to Facebook group, etc.

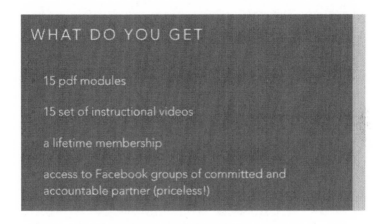

WHAT DO YOU GET

15 pdf modules

15 set of instructional videos

a lifetime membership

access to Facebook groups of committed and accountable partner (priceless!)

Step 4 – Pros and Cons

Next, mention the pros and cons of the product.

I recommend that you mention at least 4 pros for every one con.

Also, when you're writing your pros, remember to mention the benefits again as part of the pros.

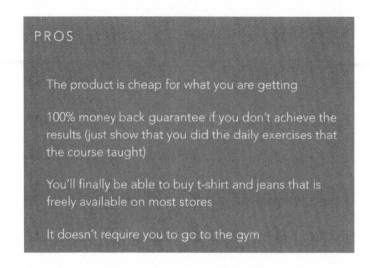

For the cons, always be honest and tell them what you didn't like about the product.

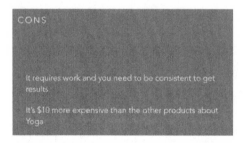

Most cons are just excuses.

E.g.

It's $10 more expensive than the average price of products in that market.

$10 won't really break the bank.

What you can do is add something like this:

Cons:

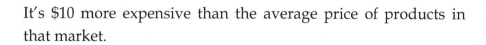
It's $10 more expensive than the other products about Yoga

ADD THIS:

However, I 100% believe that the $10 premium is worth the money. Why? Because results don't lie. I and many other people have successfully follow the training – and it just plain works!

Step 5 – Should You Get It?

The next step is to mention who should or shouldn't get the product.

Yes, you will lose some potential customers here.

But that's okay!

You want quality customers anyway.

You want the right people to buy the product.

Even if you somehow convince the wrong people. they'll just mess up and not apply the product anyway – and get refund after a few days.

Qualify them.

Let them know that not everybody should get the product.

Step 6 – Action Time

The last step is to ask them to watch the video presentation that reveals X information about your topic.

E.g.

Thanks for watching this review, if you want to learn more about how Annie loses her belly fat in less than 7 days, watch the video presentation.

Upload & Optimize the Video

You can upload your video here.

https://www.youtube.com/upload

Optimizing your video is one of the easiest and best ways to get fast rankings.

Here are some things to remember to apply so you can maximize the SEO rankings of your video on Google and YouTube.

#1 – Change Your File Name

Don't use a generic file name.

To optimize your video, change it to whatever your product name is.

E.g.

LeanBellyBreakthrough.mp4

LeanBellyBreakthroughreview.mp4

#2 – Don't Use Boring Titles

Most newbies make the mistake of using just the product name as their video's title.

Lean Belly Breakthrough Review

However, you can add some of your keywords in your title and increase your viewership reach.

Also, adding more keywords can add interest in your video so it'll get clicked in the first place.

E.g.

Lean Belly Breakthrough Review – Should You Buy It?

Lean Belly Breakthrough Review – Is it a Scam or Will It Flatten Your Stomach?

Lean Belly Breakthrough Review – The Guide to Getting Rid of Your Belly Fat

#3 – Description = Keywords

For the description…

I want you to put your affiliate link in the first line of the description.

Next, add the other keywords you are targeting as well.

E.g.

http://affiliatelink.com/one - **Lean Belly Breakthrough**

Lean Belly Breakthrough Review

Get Rid of Belly Fat

I Hate My Belly Fat

Get Rid of Stomach Fat

#4 – Put Your Tags

Put the keywords you're targeting on the tags section.

Lean Belly Breakthrough Review

Get Rid of Belly Fat

I Hate My Belly Fat

Get Rid of Stomach Fat

Then add some more as long as YouTube allows it.

#5 – Change Your Thumbnail

This one can increase the clicks to your video.

For product reviews, I recommend that you do something that is different than the other reviews already on YouTube.

Something that catches the attention of someone who's just browsing around.

Boost the SEO Rankings

You'll want to rank your keywords on both Google and YouTube.

Here are the services that you should get on Fiverr.com

SOCIAL SIGNAL

PBN LINKS

YOUTUBE EMBEDS

YOUTUBE SEO BACKLINKS

I want you get at least 1 service every 4 days.

This will help you get the #1 ranking for your keyword/s in less than 3 weeks for both Google and YouTube.

In some cases, you can see the result for as fast as 48 hours. But that depends on your keyword if it's competitive or not.

Only choose services that already have 100+ 5 star reviews.

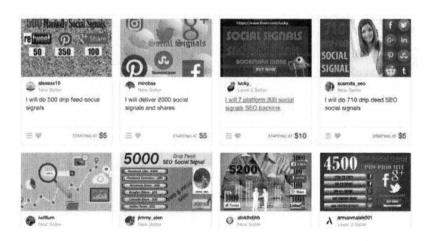

The freelancer will ask for the YouTube video url and the keyword/s you want to rank for.

Give it to em' and then let them to the work.

Conclusion

Thanks for reading this guide.

Hopefully, you'll realize that you don't need any more information to make money with affiliate marketing.

Just apply what you learned from this book and see if it works for you.

Also, don't give up too easily!

Your first product review may not make you a fortune.

Heck, even if you're already doing this for a long time, you will always have "NADA" campaigns where you'll invest $30 and your time and it won't make any money at all for a few months.

Stuff like that happens. This is a business after all.

So go ahead and do something today.

Take action and prosper!

What to Know about Earning Money with Videos

In order to successfully use YouTube to sell, you have to have a few things first.

Let's look into some physical products you must have in order to make this work, and then we can get into some digital bases you must have covered and ideas for marketing.

Products you must have to Start Earning on YouTube:

Obviously, YouTube relies on videos, so you will have to have a setup for recording videos, first and foremost. Contrary to how it may sound, this need not be elaborate or even expensive. It's perfectly possible to make professional looking videos and spend less than $1000 on your setup. Here is what your setup needs to include:

- **A Camera for Recording:** This is an obvious piece of equipment you will need. Choose a product that will shoot a minimum of 720p, or better yet, 1080p if possible. If you are going to use a webcam, Logitech is a good brand while being quite affordable. For those who would rather use a digital camera, Canon is recommended.

- **A Microphone:** A quality microphone has a large impact on the way your videos turn out. You can opt for a USB style microphone if you need to do voiceovers. If you are working with a limited budget, you can find one for less than $100. Eventually, when you earn more money, you can always upgrade to something nicer if you wish to do so.

- **The right Lighting:** Using overhead lighting that many rooms already have will cast a shadow on your videos which isn't as appealing for YouTube. You can invest in an affordable, simple setup for lighting that will give your videos a far more professional feel to them.

- **A Camera Tripod:** If you do end up using a digital camera, a tripod is a great investment. A tripod helps to make the video more stable, which isn't necessary when you're using a webcam. These can be found, typically, for less than $100, but that does depend on what type of camera you're using.

- **A Background:** Your videos can have some extra character if you have a good background. Using a sheet of large, seamless paper can work, but for more serious video makers, a background made specifically for photography will be needed, along with some fabric to go with it.

- **Software for Editing Videos:** If you're just making simple videos, extensive software for editing probably won't be necessary. A simple movie making program (like iMovie for Mac or Movie Maker for a Windows computer) should be enough. All of these products together will give you a higher chance of success.

Do you have a Website yet?

A landing page or website is a must for this, also.

Trying to earn money with YouTube without this is going to be a much slower process since YouTube is mostly useful for the traffic it can drive to your other sites. So, how do you benefit from this once you have your own store or website?

When you create videos, people need to have a link to click that will bring them to either your product page, store, or blog.

You might also want to link to your Facebook or Twitter account depending on the strategy you're using for marketing.

In each video, use a different dedicated linked page.

For example, if you have a video about how to properly pack for a trip, this can serve as a way for people to find the products you talked about in your video. Sure, this takes more work, but it leads to more results, too.

Focusing on Adding Real Value:

This sounds strange, but in order to effectively sell anything using YouTube, you have to get rid of the expectations you have of selling.

Rather, you should try to help those who view your videos by offering VALUE and ADVICE.

Sales tactics nearly never actually work in this format, *but entertainment value and good advice do.* **People don't like the feeling that someone is trying to sell them something**, so this cannot be your primary focus if you hope to have any success in this area. As soon as you've met the requirements above, you can start making videos.

Creating Engaging Video Content on YouTube

For years, video clicks were what counted in the ranking system of YouTube, that's about to change. *Instead, it will matter more how long videos* **hold the attention of viewers**...

Catchy titles or pictures as the video thumbnail are no longer enough and it will soon be mandatory to have videos that HAVE REAL VALUE TO THEM IN ORDER TO GAIN LOYAL SUBSCRIBERS AND, EVENTUALLY, CUSTOMERS.

So, how do you stay relevant in the midst of this change? Here are some tips for doing that.

Tips for Holding your Audience's Attention:

- **Who is your Audience?** This is a question you must know the answer to. You ideally should have the ability to say who your audience is, including their age range, hobbies, and interests. Which benefits are they searching for and what words are going to hold their attention?

- **Get to the Point:** Ensure that your views find out within the first few seconds why they must continue to watch your video. Tell and show them what they will gain from watching.

- **Be Energetic:** Those who show that they have energy and passion for what they're doing on their videos will be much more successful at keeping the attention of their viewers than those who are dull and monotonous.

- **Be a Risk-Taker:** As soon as you've figured out who is watching your videos, trust your intuition about them and don't be afraid to take risks. You can't just follow the path that someone else has set and expect to have great success. Instead, think like an entrepreneur.

- **Have a Script and Plan for your Content:** Your first goal in this area should be to decide what your YouTube channel is going to deliver to its audience. After that, you can start to plan out the video structure you'll be using. What do you love to create? What skills need to be developed in order to do this? Don't just try to copy whatever happens to be trending on existing channels. You will have success when you follow what you actually care about.

Having a script increases the likelihood that your video performance will go better.

Not only does it help you keep your video content organized and efficient, but it helps you stay on topic as you talk. No one likes to watch a video of someone rambling on and forgetting what they were saying every two minutes. Plan for this and make your videos well-structured.

- **Making Quality Videos:** This is an obvious one, but creating great content is a must for keeping your viewers around. Ensuring that you keep it quality throughout the whole video, and not just at the beginning, is a must for making sure that your viewers stay with you the whole time. Videos that work best will be either informative or entertaining, but the absolute best is both. This is standard knowledge for any type of marketing content, but specifically, videos should both entertain and inform to be successful.

Be Honest and Genuine:

People respond best to truth and honesty.

Just consider the obnoxious car salesman that everyone thinks is fake and mildly annoying.

You don't want to be just another salesman! Instead, show your true ideas and self in your videos, including your own sense of humor, and even some of your personal emotion. This genuine touch is what people tend to appreciate when it comes to their favorite video creators. Being fake will not get you far for long.

- **Make them Want to Return:** Make sure that your videos will both capture the audience's attention, but keep them coming back. One method for doing this is uploading videos that have a more viral type of entertainment content, but also uploading videos that you hope people will come back to again and again. For those who don't like being on film, screencasts are an option. However you decide to do it, make a policy that you only publish content that is informative and adds value to the life of those who watch it.

- **Building Incentive**: Give viewers a reason to want to come back to your YouTube page by hinting at what you will talk about in future videos or the next upload you create. This builds a sense of anticipation and will leave them thinking about what your next video will be about. This is a basic marketing strategy that all successful content creators already know about, so make sure you take advantage of this simple but effective tool and strategy. Let's look at what else you can do to increase the engagement of your viewers and video content you upload.

Having a High Upload Frequency:

People subscribe to your video channel because they like your work and hope to see more of it.

Subscribers will not appreciate a channel that doesn't put out new videos on a regular basis.

Particularly in this modern day, viewers will be hoping for more entertainment regularly, so you have to be ready to keep up with this demand.

You have to utilize consistency if you want to develop a relationship that lasts with your audience.

Try to release each video you make in a recurring, timely, and structured way, on a weekly basis if you can.

Let your viewers know that they can count on you to bring them what they like; your great content, of course!

Creating a Schedule for your Videos:

If you can't publish weekly, try for bi-weekly or monthly. Stay with your publishing schedule and try not to veer off course with it. Viewers like being able to expect when they will see a new video. This allows them to anticipate the content you will deliver and appreciate it even more when they do have access to it.

That will help you build a loyal following that returns to your channel time and time again and eventually helps you build your passive income from YouTube.

How to get More YouTube Subscribers

Content on YouTube is in the lead for marketing content in the year 2017. It's free, and while other companies try to compete with the game of video marketing, such as Twitter or Facebook, *they have had nowhere near the amount of success that YouTube has had.*

For anyone who already has a channel on YouTube, the question of whether you can earn money from it is a logical one. To do this, though, you first have to have a lot of subscribers.

How do you do this?

Keep reading

How to Increase your Subscribers on YouTube Now:

YouTube has more than a billion new visitors each and every month, meaning that there is a huge audience potential with every single video uploaded. Whether it's comedy material or makeup tutorials, YouTube is the first choice platform for viewing video content. Plenty of new stars are rising on YouTube, so it's certainly the right platform to use for people hoping to get publicity and marketing. You can use it to broaden your reach to your followers by making the connection more personal. The chance a blogger has to use this medium to their advantage and gain high levels of traffic from this site is pretty high, but first requires that you have more subscribers.

- **Cover the Details in your Script:** When you make up a script for your videos, make sure that you are as detailed as possible. Include the precise words you will use, along with the actions you'll cover in your video, along with the major points to talk about, and specific calls for your audience members to take action on. You should also know who your audience is and craft a script that is based on what they understand. Are they from America or not? Do they know about technology? Are they looking for entertainment value, or something more informative and detailed? All of these questions will help you think about who they are and use the right words to tell them what they want to know.

- **Optimizing Video Titles:** Standing out in the crowd is a must for being successful in this area, and giving your content unusual names is one way to do this. That will have people coming to see your channel or videos out of curiosity. But getting plenty of views is about more than just that.

Using SEO for Greater YouTube Success:

In order to get the most views possible, you will have to take a look at marketing and SEO. SEO stands for search engine optimization, meaning that you have a chance to show up when people search for content related to the subject you're covering on your YouTube channel. The first step of doing this is optimizing the titles you have so that they extend and reach further. Here are some basic tips for doing that:

- **Using Keywords in your Video Titles:** This used to have a bigger impact than it does now, but with video it still has a decent effect. You can use AdWords on Google to find out what it is that people are looking for online, and then try to make videos that blend together low competition and high searches.

- **Have a Shorter Title:** To have success with this, your title shouldn't be too long. Try to aim for a title that is 50 characters or less, an engaging description, and is descriptive enough, offering a preview to the content of the video. If you need more help with writing relevant, catchy, and optimized video titles, do some extra research on this topic, or simply experiment to find out what works best.

- **Using Customizations for your Channel:** If your plan is to get your audience to trust what you are selling on your channel, you need to use the options for customization that come with it. Making sure that you look professional will ensure that your viewers trust and respect what you have to say. If you have a blog already that has some followers, use similar elements of branding for your channel on YouTube so that you will be recognized on both.

This can involve using channel art that distinguishes your brand and you as a person. This is offered on YouTube for an affordable price. You could also look into having a header that is custom made and has some elements of design from the existing blog you have. Take advantage of the custom URL and channel bio sections to make this even more personalized and customized. For those who are interested, provide a blog link in your video's description.

- **Using Thumbnails:** Most creators on YouTube agree that making a custom thumbnail for their videos is better than allowing the randomly generated thumbnails. You can use relevant images and annotations as custom choices and this will improve the number of clicks you get. Adding a small annotation to your custom thumbnail will let your audience know what the video is going to cover.

- **Using a Trailer for your Channel:** YouTube gives video creators the chance to use trailers that will allow you to play a video automatically when your channel opens. The trailer you choose should be worked on carefully and improved constantly in order to keep your viewers interested and engaged. You have to use this moment to capture your viewers' attention in just seconds. Your trailer should be between half a minute and one minute, and you should give reasons why your viewers should stay on your channel and what you can offer to them.

This is obviously easier for those who are naturally comfortable with a camera. Try to give a quick, engaging, informative introduction based on a script you decided upon beforehand. You can read through the channel reports for your YouTube account, looking at the rates of viewer retention, in order to see if you are losing potential viewers with a lengthy or boring trailer. Then keep making adjustments until you have a perfect trailer.

- **Using Calls to Action:** Annotations for calling your audience to action are those little popups that come up while they are watching the video. These can lead to a higher number of subscribers by including them to click the popup while they watch your video. Many video creators on YouTube have noticed increased subscriptions to their channel when they added these. You can put in a link that encourages audience members to subscribe, or you can use a graphic. If you do this in a way that isn't annoying or obnoxious, your subscriptions will grow as a result. However, if you do this in an annoying way, you might actually lose potential subscribers.

- **Using the Correct Tools:** There is no shortage of useful tools in this area, from video creation tools to video promotion tools. Using the correct resources will aid you in growing your organic video views. When you have organic video views, you have access to a higher number of potential audience subscribers.

- **Allow People to Discover you**: YouTube gives users the choice to click a link and get sent to your website. So if you already have a website, do this as soon as possible. There is absolutely no reason not to take advantage of this option if you can. Any effort you dedicate to bringing video views to your channel can be taken advantage of any time you direct viewers to your webpage. In addition, this will make your channel a verified, authentic source for your personal brand. In your YouTube page channel settings, you can add your blog URL or website to the channel.

You could also add your URL or website to the description of your YouTube channel. You can also add a subscribe option button on your webpage or blog to bring more subscribers to your channel.

- **Make your Videos Shorter**: Your videos shouldn't be any longer than five minutes. Even though YouTube houses many in-depth, detailed reviews and longer videos, the videos that have the highest conversion rates are shorter than five minutes. Most YouTube videos are around four and a half minutes, so this is a good range to shoot for as a beginner on the site. Stick with this until you have a reliable following for your account, and then you can mix it up and experiment with different lengths later on. It can be hard to keep videos entertaining, informative, simple, and also short, but it will be well worth the effort you put in.

- **Intros and Outros**: The intros and outros you use for YouTube will aid you in branding your name and also will help your videos have a higher entertainment value. This will give your videos a professional feel and can be used as a sort of opening theme, similar to a show that people come back to and enjoy the familiarity of. In addition to this, an appealing intro ensures your audience is more involved with your videos.

- **Be a Ruthless Editor**: In order to get the best of your content out on the web, you have to make a lot of it, and edit it ruthlessly. Most creative geniuses make a lot more content than they actually show, and what we see is their best work. This should apply to your YouTube videos too. Edit them fearlessly to ensure that you are only publishing your absolute best videos. When you try to force yourself to publish on a strict schedule without taking the time to make the videos good, your brand will be hurt down the road. Make plenty of recordings for your final cut, but only publish the best. If you aren't sure about a specific take, you can always take multiple shots. If you're using Windows, Adobe Premier is a great program for editing your videos.

- **Optimizing Descriptions in your Videos**: Returning to the SEO (search engine optimization) side of making YouTube content, you should never neglect the descriptions of your videos. Your video descriptions will allow your content to be easily discovered in a search engine while also giving your potential audience members a sneak preview of what your content discusses. However, this shouldn't be overdone.

Putting a really detailed description in your video won't make any sense because the first few sentences are the only parts that are displayed when someone loads the video. Like your video's title, the keyword should be used in the video description but not overdone. You can't outsmart search engines by entering the keyword 20 times. In fact, that will likely just hurt your odds of getting displayed on search engines. Instead, make it authentic and natural.

- **Use Meta Tags for your Videos**: You can put Google's Keyword Planner to good use by finding relevant ideas to use for keywords in your videos, then adding them to your content and videos. This will allow you to be easier to discover on both YouTube and Google searches. If you overdo this, it's not going to help (and will actually do the opposite) but adding in some well-placed and researched words will help your rankings a lot.

Keep in mind that if you have a low view count on your videos, it doesn't always mean your content isn't good. It might just mean that it isn't easy to discover for viewers. Metadata plays a bit role with allowing your content to be more easily displayed to those who are searching. Look at some videos that are well-converting and look at the meta tags they have on them in order to get an idea of what works. However, don't simply copy/paste these tags because that won't work.

- **Think about How you End them**: No matter what your video content is about, you should always end videos on a high note. Similar to the very last bit of dialogue before a play ends, videos should end in a way that is memorable and positive. Ask the viewers watching to subscribe and like your video if they enjoyed it, and then ask them to visit your blog our website. Keep in mind that if you don't ask for anything, you won't get anything. End all of your content with a confident flourish, allowing viewers to know you appreciate them. End videos in a positive way, smiling and leaving your audience eager to see more content from you.

- **Think about Collaboration**: You can collaborate with other video creators on YouTube. In fact, this has turned into quite a common act among video makers. Why is that? Because when you collaborate, everyone benefits from it. Your audience benefits, the people involved in the collaboration benefit, and so do you. Creativity is all about being constructive and viewing other video creators as just your competition doesn't help. Instead, celebrate the success of others and see how you can join together to improve each other's success.

Look for successful video creators in your field and see if you can collaborate to make an interesting project. And always remember to look for what you can add to their channel as well. This will let you connect with new audience members that you may have never reached before, and the person you collaborate with will also have access to new viewers. The audience will appreciate the new value and extra content, as well. As you can see, this is an advantage for all parties involved.

- **Make sure you Interact with Viewers:** The art of social media relies on interaction and connection with people who share your common goals and ideas. This means that the amount you care directly influences your success. When the people viewing your content can tell you actually care for them as people, they will return the favor. No one wants to be involved with someone who doesn't care about them, even when they are just YouTube subscribers. Make an effort to interact with your viewers, paying attention to the requests they give you in comments.

You might get some anger or backlash in comments, but don't allow that to distract you from paying attention to your loyal listeners and viewers. When your viewers take the time to comment on your videos, make an effort to respond to what they're saying. That will build some trust between you and your audience, leading them to respect you for taking the time to connect. This is how you build a loyal fan base.

- **Do Challenges and Offer Prizes**: Who doesn't like to receive prizes or complete challenges? After you build up a loyal fan base, you can offer them some kind of compensation for staying true to your channel. A contest or prize giveaway can help you to lure in new viewers and reward those who have stood by your channel. You can give away T-shirts, a tech gadget, or a free hosting subscription. The possibilities are endless. No matter what you choose to give away, your viewers will appreciate receiving something free and will likely share this with their friends.

Not only does this give you a chance for free promotion, but possible viral promotion for your YouTube channel. For huge giveaways, some hosts on YouTube require that their audience members must subscribe to each of their social media platforms before they can enter the giveaway, which is a great approach. The prize items should be relevant to the niche your videos are about, but it's okay even if they are not.

- **Promoting Across Platforms is a Must**: In our modern social media age, being active and present across different platforms of social media is a must for succeeding and growing any type of online audience. When you are attempting to create a brand for yourself, you have to be discoverable. This means being active on more than one platform for social media. Try putting up profiles on Google Plus, Twitter, and Facebook. However, you can go further and put up Instagram and SnapChat accounts too. You can give Google and Facebook ads a try to in order to give yourself further promotion.

When you are visible throughout various platforms online, you are making yourself far more visible. Make sure that you are being aggressive about securing your first followers, which will, in turn, motivate you to create better content. You can't just build a great website and expect your customers to show up right away. Use every resource you can to build up your brand. You can also share your channel with interested friends, but try not to hassle or pester them.

- **Keep on Trying**: Experimenting and changing your methods until you find what works is the best approach anyone can take. Remember that there is never one single path to success and that what works for others might not always work best for your personal pursuits. Find what works for your brand

and channel. This could include switching up the thumbnails, backgrounds, camera angles, and other techniques given to you in this chapter. Pay attention to the way your audience changes according to these changes, and always stay true to what your brand is about.

Making something memorable and valuable on YouTube will require lots of perseverance, time, effort, and dedication from you. However, if you stick with it and stay patient, it can work for you. These are only guidelines to get you started. Don't be afraid to think outside the box and come up with your own methods!

Selling on YouTube with Affiliate Marketing

In order to start to make money from YouTube, you first have to get comfortable with making your very own, personal videos, of course. For some, this can sound easier than it really is, especially for those who are shy or nervous to be on camera,

But once you get a quality setup for recording and a few ideas going, you will start to have fun with putting content on YouTube.

The type of video content you will make will depend on what you're trying to sell, but let's get started with a few specific ideas you can test out on your YouTube channel.

Ideas for making your YouTube Video Channel more Interesting:

- **Have a Question and Answer Segment:** Your audience members and customers will probably have some questions to ask you about the product you are selling, whether it's before you sell or afterward. You can make a list of any questions they have and answer them on your channel. This is like a FAQ for your channel and will save you time on answering the same questions time and time again.

- **Show Behind the Process Scenes:** People are often interested to see the process behind manufacturing, particularly in processes involving branding. When you create a product of your own, you should show how the process of manufacturing goes, which assures your customers of what your brand is all about. It also allows them to see the quality of what you make and see the culture behind your business.

- **Topical Video Content:** FAQ type videos and behind the process videos are great, but they are limited in the potential they have to reach and entertain your audience. Content focused on topical industry information has the potential to reach a bigger viewer base, however. These videos should help your audience members gain an understanding of issues and finding solutions to them. In addition, it can focus on entertainment, knowledge, and facts. If you, for instance, sell accessories related to traveling, you could put out videos about packing efficiently, or items you might need while taking long trips. But when you want to have viral videos, try to make informative, short ones like Buzzfeed videos.

- **Involve Product User Stories:** How do real customers make use of what you sell? Interviewing your previous customers and telling their personal stories is a good idea for YouTube video content. Contact your past customers to ask them if you can use their stories for your channel. Many of them will agree wholeheartedly (particularly if their blog or business can be promoted in your video). Interview them at their place or have them come to your video studio. This works very well for branding purposes and general testimonial sharing.

- **Sharing Others' Reviews:** Finally, your channel doesn't need to be limited to only your personal videos. It should ideally include other people's content too, particularly review videos done by other YouTube video creators. These reviews can be found by searching the name of your brand or product on the website. Then ask the video blogger for permission to feature their review video on your account. The majority of bloggers will be glad for the exposure.

How do you Gain YouTube Traffic?

The next thing you need to do once the videos are made is bring video traffic either to your landing page or website. Thankfully, YouTube gives users a few different ways to let people interact with YouTube content and videos.

- **Annotations for Similar Content:** We already briefly discussed annotations in the previous chapter, but make sure that you use them to link to any videos you have on your channel that are related or similar, so users stay on your YouTube page.

- **Cards for Interaction:** Interactive cards are a new addition to the marketing tools on YouTube. These elements can be placed in your videos to perform functions such as showing websites, products, other video content, or even to raise money from within the video. In order to make use of this, read up on the help section on Google to figure out what card you can use and how.

More for Marketing and Growing your Audience:

As soon as your videos are done and uploaded, you need to keep working on promotion for your YouTube channel. Depending on the skills for marketing you already have, this could be either the hardest or easiest part of selling for you. Employ these tactics any time to get a head start, even if you are a complete beginner with marketing.

- **Get Creative with Answering Questions:** As mentioned before, engaging with your audience is a must for having a successful channel. Of course, YouTube commenters aren't always the most thoughtful or polite, but engaging with the ones that are will help your brand's success. Instead of just answering the questions of your commenters, though, try looking up videos about similar subjects created by other YouTube users. If you sell work out equipment, for example, look up related videos and leave comment responses on there. This increases your visibility.

  Please remember to never aggressively push your products. This is a strategy that plenty of people use and it nearly never works because people don't like being pressured to buy things. Instead, leave helpful hints to commenters that they can find out more about the subject by going to your videos. Your priority at this stage must always be to be offering value and help, and the money will come later on.

- **Making Relevant Titles and Descriptions:** YouTube is a wildly successful search engine (the second biggest one on the internet). In addition to being its own successful site, it dominates searches on Google too, these days. Videos are displayed in more than half of Google's search results and most of those are YouTube videos. We've already covered a bit on SEO before, but let's look at some other tips you can use to improve yours on your channel. Make sure that your video keywords already have some existing results on Google. The keywords should have at least two results already online.

  When you make your video title, make sure you use those keywords and ensure that the name of your video file also has those same keywords in it. For instance, if the name of your video is "Packing on a Trip," the title and name of the file could be "packing-trip.mp4" and "Packing on a Trip, a Detailed Guide" in addition to that. Your video description should have a length of at least 200 words to describe your video and have a positive impact on the content's SEO.

- **Think Bigger**: We talked a bit about adding your content to your other social media platforms and profiles, such as Google and Facebook. But you can take this a step further by messaging Twitter accounts and Facebook pages that are in related niches and request that they share your content. A lot of pages like that are searching for good content that they can share with their viewers and subscribers. For content of yours that is big or newsworthy, get a hold of news outlets or blogs like Huffington Post and more and ask them to share your content. You can also link to your video in community forum areas like Reddit.

- **Promotion on YouTube**: Even though you should focus on promoting your content on other sites, you should of course dedicate plenty of time to promoting your videos on YouTube itself, as well. This involves creating playlists that are optimized for SEO, so that they will show up in the pane of related videos and add to your existing views. Make a separate area requesting that people become channel subscribers for your content and put this segment into each video that you make, pointing at the subscription button with annotations.

If you do all of the steps above, you will notice that selling on YouTube, and gaining viewers, doesn't have to be a difficult chore. It should be viewed as a process that will develop over the long term, not a scheme to become a millionaire overnight. Rather, invest your time in this process and grow your audience authentically with the attitude that you want to help others and add value to the internet. Whichever future sales you do end up making later on will naturally come this way, after you have built a trustworthy and respected brand for yourself.

Using Affiliate Marketing for Earning on YouTube:

Another method people can use to earn money on YouTube, get a passive income, and eventually gain financial independence and freedom is through YouTube monetization using affiliate marketing. Affiliate marketing is when you supply links to other people's products and bring them sales through your audience members. Not only can you earn money from ad impressions left on your videos, but by putting affiliate marketing links in the video descriptions. Typically, these earn even more than video ads, plus it has the benefit of benefiting many different people. Stick with these tips if you want to be successful in this area:

- **Stick with What you Know:** If you are trying to be as general as possible in your videos in order to gain a bigger audience, cut out this strategy now. Instead, stick with what you already know! People want to hear from those who have personal experience with what they are talking about, not someone who is just trying to sell them something. If you're an artist, talk about paint supplies, if you're a fitness expert, link to books on nutrition or exercise clothes and equipment.

- **Be Relevant:** For this to work well, you do have to make sure you plan right. For example, only link to relevant products that have to do with the subject you're discussing in the video. Otherwise, it will just come across as confusing. Doing this also gives you the benefit of an audience who is more likely to be interested in what the link is selling, follow it, and buy something.

- **Get People to View:** As soon as you have some affiliate links in your video descriptions, you should just work on getting more views, which you are probably already working on! In order to be even more successful in this, get some of your content uploaded and then work on becoming a partner on YouTube. This gives you an added chance to have higher ranked videos. If you don't know what kind of videos you should make, there are plenty of articles online giving out free ideas for this.

Some affiliate marketing opportunities will pay you for every click you get on their product link, while others require that the people actually buy something before you get any earnings from it. The best part is that, either way, you are earning income completely passively just by having the link there on your video description. Seek out products relevant to your niche and find what works for you to benefit from this method of earning on YouTube.

Using AdSense on YouTube

YouTube is a great stream for revenue, and this is true for many different companies and businesses. However, incoming money is usually small when you only have a small audience. Sure, you can monetize your video content without using AdSense. However, the properties linked with Google will allow you the extra advantage of having everything you need in one place (a single control panel). AdSense is a great resource and tool, especially for people who already know how to use it. Linking up your YouTube and AdSense accounts is very simple, but it might require some waiting time for Google to process and approve your application.

How can you Link your Existing AdSense and YouTube Accounts?

When you already have an approved account with AdSense, and you have a YouTube account that qualifies to be monetized, you will find the process of linking them together painless and very simple. Here are the steps:

- Go to the page for your channel settings in your YouTube account, then access the monetization option. This should bring you to a section on How to get Paid.

- Find the Association page on AdSense and go through the steps it gives you for going to AdSense. Continue and use your Google account to login. It must be the one that you are using with your YouTube channel.

- Click "Accept" for the association with AdSense and let your internet browser get redirected back to the YouTube page.

This is all you have to do. By now, Google will need to go through and process the request you just entered, which might take a couple of days to go through. As soon as this is activated, you can manage ads on YouTube using AdSense from Google, taking advantage of the control and analytics that come along with it. The steps for monetizing your videos when you don't yet have an account with AdSense are basically the same as this.

You need to go to your settings in the channel and visit monetization settings. But then once you get redirected over to AdSense, you have to create an account on AdSense. This does take a little longer than the steps listed above, but it's pretty simple to figure out. You can also follow these instructions to edit any settings you need in this area.

Restrictions for Monetization:

There are, of course, restrictions to this, as well.

YouTube doesn't let people monetize any content.

Your videos only qualify if you are the owner of all rights to what the video includes, on a worldwide and commercial level.

What this means is that your content can't have content that you don't own selling rights to or completely own yourself.

Your videos have to abide by the terms of service and YouTube's community guidelines.

Although this seems easy enough, there are a few things that might ruin your video's eligibility. Let's look at some of these flags that mean you cannot upload the video:

- Any video with background music that is copyrighted, live performances of copyrighted information, or specific sound files that are commercial.

- If your video has logos from any businesses that aren't yours, this is a restriction that means you don't own full rights to the video content. This also applies to videos with software that is not your own within them.

- Media property, video game, or movie footage that you don't own the rights to also disqualifies you from using that video for monetization.

All of this can be a bit complicated, particularly when it comes to the modern day copyright laws,

For instance, you can't use songs for your video content, even if you did by the song to listen to yourself. You first have to get a commercial license if you wish to use it beyond your own personal listening purposes, which can't always be done at all.

Image Complications and Rules to Adhere to:

Another restriction you should think about is stock images.

You can of course use images within your video content, but you need to own the rights to that image every time. This means images that you yourself have created or that your business owns, like your business logo.

Any images that you have bought to use commercially from a site that hosts stock images are fine, as well, but you can't just pull any photo you find on Google images and use it in your videos.

Sure, there are countless YouTube videos that have game feeds, movie footage, or audio that the video content creator doesn't own, and sometimes these are monetized videos. But this is usually because either YouTube doesn't know about it or hasn't discovered any violations yet, or because there is some legal gray area included.

- **Better Safe than Sorry:** Just remember that in order to be safe and avoid headaches down the road, just buy the necessary licenses for what you use in your videos. This can damage your reputation and channel if you don't take these precautions and play it safe while you can.

- **Manual or Automatic Penalties:** Violating any copyrights can lead to either a manual or automatic YouTube penalty. In either case, it's hard to get rid of this type of violation or remove the record of it. Even worse than that, you will have a hard time monetizing your content down the road. If you did violate these rules, your account won't be allowed to be monetized again in the future.

The Analytics of YouTube:

For users of YouTube who are more experienced, but new to monetizing, perhaps you have noticed a new area of information in the analytics suite area on the site. This covers the estimated and existing earnings suite. Using that, you can visualize the trends of both your past and current trends, along with an estimation of future earnings according to your current trends and performance. Having this information will give you a huge leg up, and staying on top of how well your videos are doing is a must. Remember that the reports for estimated earnings on YouTube are only visible when you have your account on AdSense already linked.

Thresholds of Payment:

When you earn on YouTube, you have to give your personal tax info as soon as you can get payments.

This means anything above 10 dollars. As soon as you've earned that much, you have to verify any information of yours for YouTube, along with your phone number and address.

Asking for Donations:

A more direct way to earn through YouTube is to simply ask for donations. This can be done either directly on your videos, or by linking a "Go Fund Me" account to your YouTube by entering the link into your video descriptions. Some people will have success with this, while others won't.

Only you can decide whether that method is right for you.

A Profitable YouTube Business Model

The "YouTube Partner" makes it possible for its associates to make money for each and every view they earn or subscriber they gather on their site. There have been people who quit their jobs and switched over to make full time videos.

1. You need to set up an account on YouTube. While setting up an account, you need to take into account the keywords that you would certainly like to include to help potential subscribers find you. In the case that you enjoy playing video games, then video games could be a great keyword – along with controllers, PlayStation, etc....

2. You need to invest in good web cam equipment. They are reasonably priced and widely available. As you get better at filming, upgrade your equipment.

3. You need to set up a Google AdSense account. From this, you will make a profit through people clicking on ads from your video.

4. Remember, you need to ask your viewers to subscribe and follow you. The more subscribers, the

more money. So it is absolutely necessary to ask for subscribing at the end of every video.

The most flourishing You Tuber's didn't get all those riches overnight. It took them years of enthusiasm and commitment to build up a firm fan base. You must utilize Twitter, Facebook, Pinterest and other social media sites to build up the subscriber base. According to socialnewsdaily.com, the top 1000 YouTube channels have an income of average roughly $23,000 a month.

YouTube is likely to earn the advertising revenue of approximately $5 billion this year. The question is how do the YouTubers get a share of that? In the end, it is their content that attracts the advertisers to this platform. Let us look at some ways of which you can generate money on this site:

Become a YouTube Partner.

Anyone having internet access has the capability to upload videos on YouTube. However, in order to make money off that content, you would be required to get enrolled as YouTube partner.

Nowadays, any person with a good account standing is eligible to become YouTube partner. They just need to give explicit permission to YouTube to place advertisements around, in and on your video. These ads views obtain money for Google.

Partners in return earn a share through an account on Google AdSense. The capacity to earn money is precisely dependent on various factors.

Go to 'Channel Settings' page

On this page go to 'Account Monetization' section

Click 'Enable My Account' tab

Once your request is approved, you would be on the way to make money from your videos.

You should be prepared for the issues in getting approvals, in case your content violates any copyright agreement or you publish any material which is sexually explicit, racist or abusive. Google will remove all such content. This can even impact the standing of your account.

Earning of YouTube Partners from the Revenues of Advertising

YouTube captures approximately 45% share of the revenues earned via advertising, even though the cost (also known as CPM) charged to the advertisers varies. Most partners earn in the range of $0.30 CPM to $2.50 CPM, however there may be exceptions. Due to these exceptions larger YouTube players, the earning capacity is now approximately $10 CPM for them.

Earnings of Partners from Merchandise or Sponsorship Deals

A lot of well-liked YouTubers have secured profitable deals of sponsorship with brand names. This is just for the reason that these creators have generated a significant audience. Moreover, they are in the correct place at the correct time. Agreements of Sponsorship are completed outside of YouTube and may take a long procedure with the sponsorship company.

Earnings of Partners from the Subscription of Paid Channels

In 2013, YouTube announced the launch of a subscription service of channels which are paid. This allowed publishers & creators to charge for the video content they upload. They also launched 53 channels with monthly charge in the range of $0.99 to $6.99.

Bigger Incomes with MCNs.

MCN is referred to as Multi Channel Networks. In the past few years, a rapid rise of MCN has been observed. These are created in certain ways to assist creators and also to build more attractive offering for monetization. These MCN's are certain independent companies who combine multiple YouTube channels. They provide support for YouTubers on the topics of copyright management, programming, promotion, enhanced earnings and collaboration.

MCNs are in a situation to offer higher earnings. This is because they are commanding superior rates of advertising rates via direct sales of ads, packaging and sponsorships.

Finally, it is clear that one can make a living from YouTube, however as with any creative enterprise, the smarter you work, the more optimized your videos are, and the better you are at marketing the more likely you'll be able to make money. Your ability to maximize your YouTube income will increase with each video that you upload. Initially, it will seem like you are wasting your time, but if you persevere, the rewards are very attractive.

What it Takes to be Successful at YouTube

Starting a new YouTube channel is not an easy task; however follow these tips on starting a channel and you will surely gain a devoted audience!

Describe "Success" as a YouTuber

Before uploading your first work, make sure you truly understand the reason for behind the YouTube channel and why you created it:

"Providing value for your audience while earning a profit from them"

Whatever the reason may be for starting this YouTube channel, you should recognize your outlook and how you define "success". This would provide you with a goal to aim towards. This will also push and persuade you to attain that goal. Having a goal that was tough to achieve would only serve to demotivate you. Set your goals as small achievable targets and you will be able to reevaluate your position when these goals are met. If you set your initial goal as "I want to make $1 million", very few broadcasters will achieve this. However, if you set your first goal as "I want 100 viewers on one of my broadcasts", this is much more achievable and will serve as motivation to achieve this goal.

Recognize Your Viewers

Knowing your audience is the key to the success of your YouTube channel. This means, you need to familiarize yourself with the audience who would be interested in viewing the videos you upload. It is crucial to understand the interests and hobbies of your target audience.

Once you are familiarized with your audience, you could then produce the videos relevant to their needs. Remember, the significance of your video is directly proportional to the viewership and subscription of your channel. You can glean a lot of information about your viewers from the comments they leave on your YouTube videos but this doesn't really give a full profile of your viewers. Thankfully, YouTube provides you with the tools to analyze this information. This will be covered in a later chapter.

Being Passionate on the Content you are Creating

Starting a YouTube channel just because you assume that it would benefit you financially is meaningless. There are a lot of different platforms that can help you earn money, however, if you don't have the zeal for it, your viewers would just have a glimpse of it and straight away identify that you're not passionate about it.

Not just that, if you are not really passionate about this task that you're doing, you would not have any internal drive to do it day in and day out. You need to believe in the content you are delivering. If you give the persona that you aren't really that interested, this is going to put the viewer in the same mindset and reduce the chances of them returning to your channel in future.

Being Knowledgeable on the Content you are Creating

Being passionate about a subject is one thing but if you don't have an in-depth knowledge of what you are presenting, your content is going to be very shallow and will not hold the attention of your audience. You need to convince the audience that you are a specialist on your subject and that they are going to learn something that they didn't know before they viewed your broadcast.

It is highly likely that you will get questions about your broadcast in the comments section of your page so you need to be able to provide comprehensive answers to these questions so that you earn the respect of your audience.

Attitude should be Positive

Audience and subscribers need a story that has a "feel good" factor, therefore just concentrate on the positivity. Keep away from complaints and constant rages. Rather, "look on the brighter side."

That is not to say that you can't highlight any issues or faults with what you are presenting but you must stay calm at all times and refrain from saying anything that could be deemed as libelous or illegal.

Constant rages may get you a reputation that will attract some subscribers, just to see you "go off on one", however this will hurt your brand and ultimately, your ability to earn.

Even though you know your subject, you must be careful so as not to come across as arrogant. Be humble and assume that the viewer has some intelligence and understanding of what you are telling them. There is nothing worse as a viewer than being made to feel inadequate by a condescending presenter.

Be Confident in your Presenting Skills

So you are passionate about your subject and you have enough knowledge to be called a specialist in your field, but these qualities will be lost if you haven't got the presentation skills to convey your knowledge to your viewers.

Getting your voice to a tone and volume that you are happy with could take a lot of time if you are not used to giving presentations or public speaking. This is one skill that you will need to hone before you can even consider publishing your first video. The way your voice comes across will say a lot about you and your channel so speak clearly, speak slowly and speak confidently.

Your Channel should be different

To make a unique channel amongst the numerous people who are willing to start a channel, you need to be different, unique and novel. Think of vast ideas and thoughts and stick to them. Views on your YouTube videos might be low in the beginning, but if you target one particular area, one section of people, you would get a huge advantage in the long run in comparison to covering a lot of areas in one go. This would also help you differentiate your channel.

If you can find a niche area of the market and your broadcasts are of sufficient quality, you really could get a massive viewer base. This is a fine line however. If you go for something too unique, there are not going to be enough viewers who are interested in your content so do your research before decided on a final subject area. Make use of the YouTube search facility to see how many other channels are out there similar to the one that you are proposing to create. If you do manage to find any, make a note of how many views they receive and then determine as to whether you think you could make a better job of securing viewers.

Connecting with Other creators:

The most essential tip for a YouTube creator is to connect, network and make connections with other YouTube creators in their niches.

By connecting with other creators who share similar interests, you are more likely to pick up some of their viewers which will be vital in the early days of your channel's life. You are starting from scratch so need to get viewers into your channel through any means possible. What better way that to target people who you already know have some interest in the material you will be broadcasting?

Make positive comments on the videos of creators of similar subjects to your own. Give these comments some substance rather than just saying "nice video". This will get you known to viewers who may then click on your profile and watch some of your videos. Hopefully they will like them enough to hit that subscribe button.

The life of YouTube is simple but not easy

It's significant to know that being actually successful and effective on YouTube is simple however it is not easy. There would be hindrances and failures. Those eager to build a well-liked channel on this platform should be tolerant, constant, and optimistic. They also need to have an open-mind for continuous learning.

There will be days when, for one reason or another, one of your broadcasts flops and doesn't get the number of viewers you expected. This could be down to a number of factors, but the important thing is not to let it get you down. If the trend of diminishing viewers continues then you will obviously need to change your approach to broadcasting and self-promotion.

In fact, the YouTube broadcaster will need to reinvent themselves several times to ensure that their approach stays fresh and that viewers are not subjected to the same format for each broadcast. Once you've done the hard work in engaging a viewer, you need to go the extra mile in order to keep them.

How to Monetize your Videos the right way

There are multiples ways for you to monetize your videos on YouTube. While using Google AdSense is the easiest way to earn, there are other methods that can bring larger profits. We will discuss some of the more popular options in this section.

Using Google AdSense

As a YouTuber, Google AdSense is probably your primary earning option. Google AdSense is the ad publishing arm of the search engine giant. Through this service, Google allows content publishers (website owners and YouTubers) to include ads to their content. The content publishers are paid based on the number of impressions or clicks that the ads get on their content.

YouTube Google AdSense Requirements

To be able to add Google AdSense to your YouTube channel, you will need to apply to the YouTube Partner Program. In the past, YouTube creators needed at least 10,000 lifetime views to be a part of the program. This was changed back in January of 2018.

The YouTube Partner Program now requires creators to have 4,000 hours of watch time within the past year (12 months) plus 1,000 subscribers. You will not see the monetization option on your channel or your account until you have reached this view and subscriber requirements. If you have a new channel, it's best to just start creating videos and building your viewership in the beginning to slowly, but surely, reach these requirements.

You will also need to make sure that your account is in good standing with YouTube. This means that you will need to avoid posting about content prohibited in the platform. This includes copyrighted content, as well as content with pornography, drug use, and excessive violence. For a complete rundown of the types of topics prohibited in the platform.

When you have reached these views and subscriber requirements, type "youtube account monetization" on Google to apply for monetization:

(https://www.youtube.com/account_monetization)

In this page, you will be able to start the monetization process. As mentioned above, the option to start monetizing will only be visible to you if you have reached the said requirements.

Applying for AdSense:

When your account is eligible for monetization, you will see an option to enable AdSense on your videos. Only accounts in good standing will be able to apply. If your account is not in good standing, an email will be sent to you that will state the reasons why you aren't accepted in the Partner Program. Don't worry if this happens because you can simply correct the issues pointed out by YouTube's monetization team and reapply. You may do this by removing or editing the videos that were flagged by the monetization team.

After correcting any issue you may have with your account, you should be accepted in the Partner Program. When this happens, you should be able to create an AdSense account or add an existing AdSense account to your channel. You can do all this in the monetization page given above.

Is this method for you?

YouTube advertising is easy to set up but the amount of revenue you will get from it can be volatile. One month, you may get as much as a few hundred dollars while on other months you may get revenues as small as $10.

The good news is that you can get into this method of earning as long as you achieve the views and subscriber count requirements. Once in, you will want to keep working on your channel to keep the ad revenue flowing. If possible, try to release one video per day. Realistically, you can only pull of this level of productivity if you create vlogs and top 10 lists. If you are aiming for higher quality videos however, you may not be able to reach the 1 post per day quota.

It is also important to note that you can only maximize your income potential in ad revenue if you create videos that are longer than 10 minutes. You can only put the maximum amount of ads into your videos if they are 10 minutes long or longer. This is extremely difficult to achieve on a regular basis.

Other Monetization Options:

Because of the more difficult views and subscriber requirements to apply for the YouTube Partner Program, it is harder for beginners now to monetize their videos with Google Ads. Don't worry though, because there are other options available for you. Here are some of the most successful monetization methods that can be used together with YouTube:

Affiliate Marketing

Affiliate marketing is the practice of selling the products of other people or business online. To become an affiliate marketer, you will need to apply to an affiliate marketing program of a brand, company, or product that you would like to promote.

Amazon.com is the biggest affiliate program in the English speaking side of the internet. It is also one of the best affiliate programs for beginners. Let's say that you are hosting a travel channel. On your travel videos, you show certain products that you use. You could then tell your users that you have an Amazon Affiliate Link in the description of your video if they like the videos.

If your viewers choose to buy the product after clicking on the affiliate link, you will earn a commission from the sale. This is an effective way to earn online when you aren't a YouTube partner yet. Some people even earn bigger revenue from their affiliate programs than their ad revenue.

Is this method for you?

Affiliate marketing is a great way to earn. However, it may not be an effective earning method for some people. For instance, comedy channels often do not have products to promote even though they get tons of views. This method of earning will work for you if your videos contain interesting products that viewers may be interested in.

Some types of channels that effectively use this type of monetization method are review channels, tutorial channels, and travel and lifestyle channels (vlogs).

Video Sponsorship

If your channel is getting a lot of monthly views, some companies or individuals may become interested in sponsoring your videos. With this monetization method, sponsors pay you money upfront before you create the video. They will then need to specify how they want their brand to be presented. Some would say for instance that they want their brand to be shown at the beginning of the video for at least 5 seconds.

If you and the sponsor agree on the terms of the transaction, you could mention the sponsor in your video according to their specified criteria.

To attract sponsors to invest in your YouTube channel, you will need to have a well-established YouTube account. Your account needs to have enough videos and at least 20,000 views each month with a steadily growing subscriber base.

To check if your channel is good enough for a sponsor, you could go to FameBit.com. Look for the section "Creators":

(https://famebit.com/creators)

FameBit is sort of a marketplace that allows YouTube creators and sponsors to meet. FameBit acts like a middleman that makes it easier for creators to find sponsors for their channel. Creators need to apply to the sponsor programs listed in the channel. If they fit the requirements of the sponsors, they may apply to the program. Their application will then be reviewed. If accepted, the creator can start creating videos for their sponsors.

As your channel becomes bigger, sponsors may seek you out. Make sure that you have a publisher communication channel for them to reach you.

Is this method for you?

Sponsorship works best if you tackle a specialized type of content that few other channels talk about or if you get a big enough following in a niche that has a lot of marketing potential. Fashion vloggers and sports-related channel both get sponsorship opportunities. For fashion vloggers, the potential sponsors are usually make up and apparel brands. App developers like SeatGeeks dominate the sponsorship offers among sports channels.

If you are creating videos about academic subjects, you may also find sponsors in the online learning niche. Udemy and SkillShare occasionally sponsor YouTube videos.

Selling your own products (Merchs)

You will also see a lot of YouTubers selling their own "merchs" (short for merchandise"). This method of earning is usually used by creators who cannot earn using the other options discussed in this chapter. While there is a potential for earning a lot with this method, it is more difficult to set up compared to the other options above. With advertising and affiliate marketing, you only need to sign up with already established programs to start. By selling your own merchandise, you will need to find a company who will manufacture your items and deliver them to potential buyers.

Selling "merchs" also tend to be expensive to your users. In most cases, it will only be a viable business option if you already have a big following on YouTube as well as in your other social media accounts.

On the positive side, selling merchs means that you will have a lion's share of the profits from your business. The same cannot be said with affiliate programs and ad publishing. If it works for your niche, consider setting up your own line of merchandise in the future.

Is this method for you?

Merchandise sale is best used with certain niches. The biggest YouTubers for instance mostly use this kind of monetization method because they have millions of loyal subscribers. This especially works if your market tends to be kids and teens. Pewdiepie and the Paul Brothers both use Merch sale to increase their revenue stream because it works with their demographics.

If you are planning to create a channel that targets these types of audiences, you may also use merchs as a way to earn. This market however, is very competitive because you are competing with every postpubescent YouTuber who is trying to become the next Pewdiepie.

Integrating YouTube Marketing

If you have other business, you may also use YouTube as a supplementary marketing tool. Millions of people around the world have a habit of going to YouTube every day to watch videos on their free time. For most people, YouTube has replaced the nightly TV habit.

You can gain access to the great number of users who may be interested in your business by creating videos that are related to your business niche. You could then leave a link to your business website in your video description. Many online companies are already using this method. For them, YouTube is another source of traffic like Google Search, Facebook, and Twitter.

Here are some of the types of videos you can create:

- **How-to videos/Tutorials:**

Some people go to YouTube to learn skills. Any company can make use of this habit to get their brands in front of people.

Some YouTube users go to YouTube for their daily dose of news on the topics they are interested in. You can also use this habit as a way to introduce your own business to people. A financial consultancy for instance could have daily news rundown videos created to engage with YouTube users. They could then have their brand visible from start to finish of the video. This kind of strategy works for industries where news viewing is extremely important like politics, finance, and show business.

- **Industry Q and A Videos and Podcasts:**

Experts can use YouTube as a way to establish themselves as persons of authority in their respective fields. Modern thought leaders like Neil DeGrasse-Tyson and Jordan Peterson for example, have made regular people interested in their academic subjects through social media and YouTube. If you are an expert in your business niche, you can create talk shows related to your niche on YouTube. You could set up a podcast and air them live in your own website as well as on YouTube.

You could also set up a Q and A video. Q and A videos (short for questions and answers) are videos where in experts answer questions asked by fans. These types of videos allow you to discuss some of the frequently asked questions in your industry. Ideally, you want to answer beginner related questions in these videos so that you will be able to reach a greater range of audience with them. You could then, direct your viewers to your website or to your stores for consultation.

Retarget your website visitors with YouTube ads

You could also use YouTube advertising to engage with potential customers or clients. For instance, you could use Google's remarketing ads to target people who have been to certain pages in your website. You could then use YouTube video ads to get these people's attention.

YouTube ads are unique because of the level of engagement that they get compared to other types of online ads. It's almost impossible for users to develop ad blindness with YouTube ads. Ad blindness happens when users become so accustomed to ads that they habitually ignore them when they appear. This is common among banner ads online.

With YouTube, ad blindness is lessened because the ads are shown when the users are most engaged. If the ad is perfectly targeted to the right users and video content, you may be able to get some additional customers or clients.

Before you go all out on using Google Ads on YouTube however, make sure to test it out first. Go to the Google Ads homepage to get started:

https://ads.google.com/

How to Build a Successful YouTube Channel

For building a flourishing and successful YouTube channel would require a plan before you begin to start creating. In absence of a plan you might end up lost half way through:

1. *Describe Yourself –What you're into, Who Are You and how you are willing to showcase yourself.*

Think about your favorite YouTube creator. Think why you liked them? Why you came back to view their content again and again? Well, this is because they have developed an exceptional individual branding which you like and enjoy. Describing yourself and building your own "personal brand" is an important aspect in the preservation and creation of YouTube channels which are successful.

You need to try to keep your concentration on something you are knowledgeable or passionate about. You need to sit down patiently and prepare a list of all the things that you love and enjoy doing. What are the things that make you feel happy?

1. *High Quality Content*

Content that has the greater production quality will tend to get a lot of shares and views. However, high quality production can be done by seeking assistance from experts. High quality content does not necessarily mean high cost. Most home users already have the equipment to being creating high quality content. The biggest factor that determines whether content will be classed as high quality will be you. If you come across well in your video and present in a style which keeps the viewer interested, your video will be perceived as being high quality. The fact that you don't have the best camera and the best microphone will be overlooked.

2. Research Your Viewers – Who are they and what is the best way to reach them?

A good association with your viewers is an important aspect of YouTubing

Building a healthy relationship with your audience is the key to your failure or success on this platform. Whatever you do should be done to build up your audience. You should always be available and approachable to them. You can get a Facebook or Twitter page and respond when they send a message to you. Be kind and always provide value. Remember that the chances of your content getting shared would be higher if more viewers have a good relationship with you.

When you build a relationship with your viewers, you get to know them more – their age, profession, gender, location etc.

This is also termed as demographic information. This information would help you develop your future content and what they want to see. Building up a profile of your viewers is a key area in running a successful YouTube channel. We'll discuss this in more detail later on in this book.

3. *Make a to-do-list and follow it*

Keep in mind that having regular and strong content is more important than having mind-blowing and irregular content. Having steady content will assist you in developing a connection with your viewers more easily, and it keeps your audience's attention and gives them more opportunities to share your valuable content. In case the gap between the videos are too long, your viewers may get uninterested and might even move to someone else.

Viewers are indecisive like that. Prepare a planner for yourself. Make it an important aspect of your day-to-day life.

If your content is not time specific (your broadcast isn't reliant on recent events), you could even record all of your content for a period of time in one sitting. This would ensure that you would always release your next video on the specified date that you said you would. The following week, you would release the next video and so on. This would guarantee regularity which would be appreciated by viewers of your channel.

5. Brand your channel header so that viewers remember your page

When you create your YouTube channel, it will be created with a generic, lifeless header. Unless the content creator changes this header themselves, you are going to have the same, boring header as the majority of casual YouTubers. This is obviously going to be an issue as you move forward as you need to draw people into your content and make your channel memorable at first sight. Creating channel art is a simple process but before diving straight into it, it is worth thinking about your channel header as this will be the first impression that viewers get about you and your channel.

Channel art can you selected from any image you have on your computer or you can elect to use something generic from the YouTube gallery. If you are going for the wow factor or branding that tells the viewer about yourself or your channel's purpose, you are going to need to create your own unique header in a package such as Photoshop.

Once you are happy with your header, you can upload it onto your YouTube channel. YouTube will then show you how your channel header will look on computer, TV and mobile versions of your channel. This will give you the opportunity to make any alterations you wish to, before your new header goes live. Once you are happy, simply save the changes and your new header will be visible to all users.

Although the addition of channel art is a really quick process, it is vitally important to get it right. Of course, channel art can be changed at any time and it is encouraged periodically as this gives the perception that you are constantly updating the content and freshness of your channel which most viewers will welcome. Be careful not to use any logos from other companies otherwise you may find yourself in violation of the terms of the AdSense program which could make you ineligible to earn any money from your YouTube channel.

Tips for a Successful YouTube Channel

Please know that the Most Engaging YouTube Videos are Global, Funny, and touching.

Just Get Started

Firstly, you need to create an account. In case you are already holding an account with Gmail, you can simply login with the same username and password. Though, it's useful to create a separate email address, so you can consider making a fresh account dedicated to your channel. Think very carefully about the user name while making an account- as this will effectively become your product name, so you need to make sure that it's something you are actually passionate about. Try to avoid user names which may be considered as offensive. It is also important to create a user name that will stand the test of time. If your channel is going to stand the test of time, giving it a name of something which is current now, but will be outdated in 12 to 18 months is going to be counter-productive. This is a common mistake that casual YouTube content creators make.

Content Is Key

Please know that your YouTube content is king. YouTube has lately updated its feature called "video discovery" to keep an attention on the watch time vs. number of views.

Before registering an account, you need to sketch out a plan. You need to think about the kind of content you want to create. When planning your content, plan for several weeks in advance if possible. New users have a tendency to put all their good ideas into their first broadcast which is wrong for so many reasons. Firstly, as you are a new broadcaster, it is highly likely that your first broadcast is going to be seen by very few people. Putting all of your high quality content and ideas into this broadcast will mean that they will only be seen by a small audience and you will not get the level of impact you desired.

Another reason not to put too many of your good ideas into one broadcast is that viewers will come to expect that level of quality each time you broadcast. If you have delivered a high quality, innovative broadcast the time before, but on your latest broadcast, you have run out of ideas, the viewer is going to get bored very quickly and either unsubscribe from your channel or just not bother viewing as regularly which is not the kind of viewer experience we want to deliver.

Unless your channel is planning to deliver breaking news, it is usually possible to plan for a couple of months of weekly broadcasts. Think of this like a TV series. For each individual broadcast, concentrate solely on one subject. This will allow viewers to absorb information far more easily than if you discuss multiple subjects. At the end of your broadcast, you want your viewer to be embellished with knowledge rather than being confused because they have had too much information thrown at them. You should always close your broadcast by summarizing what you have covered in your video so that the viewer is clear what they have just watched. This will allow them to take away key points rather than thinking it was all just a blur.

At the end of each broadcast, it is your job as a broadcaster to try and entice the viewer back for your next broadcast. This is quite a skill to master as you will need to use different methods each broadcast to prevent your style from becoming stale. It is your job to make your next broadcast sound interesting and appealing to the viewer. You almost need to get them to convince themselves that they cannot afford to miss the next broadcast. If you have already recorded the next broadcast, maybe a quick snippet could be shown as a teaser.

Viewer retention is one of the key factors in running a successful YouTube channel. Getting views to believe in what you are doing and to buy in to your project is very difficult to master and may not happen straight away. You will need to experiment with different approaches to see which one works best for you.

Also, YouTube requires you to opt for a category that will define your interest topic. Few examples of the categories are, beauty, entertainment, comedy, cooking, education, and music.

Be Unique and Novel

YouTube says that to get entitled for monetization, "you must possess all the required rights to make use of all audios and visuals commercially, irrespective of whether they are yours or of a third party." Copyright videos and audios of any other YouTuber do not meet the criteria for earning money.

Before choosing your content for making money, you need to assure that you have the required basic rights to exercise the content for making profits and that you will include the background melody.

This is an important condition that most YouTube content creators are unaware of until it is too late. If you upload a video of your cat doing cute things (a common YouTube theme) but put this video to your favorite tune by your favorite artist, you will immediately be ineligible for any remuneration for this video. Even though you own the rights to the video, you have violated YouTube's copyright policy by using someone else's audio.

Unless your broadcast is going to contain voice only then this could be a problem to the majority of broadcasters. An easy way to remember a YouTube broadcaster is by the theme music that leads into their video. If you had an idea of using a catchy 30 second snippet from one of your favorite artists, you will need to think again. If you are unable to create a theme that represents your brand well enough, don't do it, just go straight to the main content of your broadcast. Remember, content is king. A good theme tune may make your channel more memorable but a bad one will certainly have a negative effect and could potentially drive viewers away if your channel is perceived as being amateur by the choice of theme music.

Whilst on the subject of the terms and conditions for which you can earn money from YouTube, under no circumstances must you ever click on an advert that is displayed on one of your YouTube videos. Google take a dim view of this and often class it as a way to defraud advertisers. Initially you may get a warning but Google have the power to disable your AdSense account for life. Without this, your earning capability is zero so it is really not worth the risk. There will be plenty of other viewers who will be more than happy to click the links for you.

Patience and Steadiness

Don't expect your video to go viral overnight. You need to be consistent and provide value constantly in order to start earning those valuable views. The majority of filmmakers on this platform have times where they don't feel like creating a video, however subscribers desire dependability. They wait for a video from your end on a regular basis, so don't expect victory if you post your videos only when you want to. Remember to post constantly, which will get your channel noticed.

Although regular posting is essential to gain traction with YouTube viewers, you must be in the right frame of mind to post. If you post on the same day each week, but in one particular week, you don't feel up to it, hold on for tomorrow. Viewers would rather wait an extra day to see you at your best than to see you on time but just going through the motions. If you actually make a visual appearance in your videos, body language is crucial in getting over your message to the viewer. If they can see that you are not enjoying the performance, they will be less inclined to believe the message that you are trying to get across. Although this may be less of a factor if you are only doing a voiceover in your broadcast, viewers will still pick up negative vibes if your voice is in a slightly different tone to the one that they expect.

If you are constantly late in delivering content to viewers then your reputation will eventually suffer. However, once every now and then will not be a problem. Most viewers will be understanding, especially if an apology is offered at the start of your broadcast for it being slightly late. There are also positives to be taken from a late broadcast. If a viewer is disappointed that one of your broadcasts is late, this means that they do indeed look forward to what you have to broadcast. Although you don't want to make a habit of being late, you've got this viewer hooked, for now!

If your content is really exceptional, you may get away with broadcasting to a flexible schedule where your posts can appear at any time on any day with no set pattern. This is not advisable for new broadcasters as you need to establish a dedicated viewer base in order to secure views before you will be afforded this luxury. If you start off using a flexible schedule, you will find that there will be no pattern to your views. Some videos will receive a reasonable amount of views whereas others will receive a low amount, simply because people are not clear as to when your content is being delivered.

Encourage *Yourself*

Know that even the best content needs endorsing to get listed in the "most popular" category listing. You need to link your YouTube channel with Twitter, Google+ and Facebook to automatically put your content to numerous accounts once you've uploaded.

Viewers would like to get engaged with your content. Use social media to connect with your audiences and ask for ideas for an upcoming video in order to get audience engagement, which will make them feel part of your community. You are encouraged to use as many social media sites as possible to promote your content. As long as you don't spam these sites, you will see a difference in your viewing figures by engaging viewers in this way. We'll discuss more about self-promotion later on.

Equipment:

You need to know that to keep up a flourishing YouTube channel, you don't need thousands of dollars. High quality cameras are now available for at reasonable prices — and most YouTube users have created convincing content by simply filming with a use of a phone.

With HD webcams now standard, internal broadcasts where the broadcaster is in a static location and is either talking to the camera or demonstrating a skill or product can be created with next to no expense at all. As long as the camera is secured correctly so that it is not wobbling every time the broadcaster moves, a webcam represents the easiest way of creating your content.

One issue that often gets overlooked when creating broadcasts is the sound quality. As most recent webcams now include a built in microphone, a lot of home broadcasters assume that this will give them sufficient quality when broadcasting. Unfortunately, the majority of built-in webcam microphones give a tinny output which, while it is OK for Skype, is not really sufficient for creating a professional broadcast for YouTube. To get the best audio quality for a relatively low price, it is advisable to go for a USB microphone and a pop screen which will eliminate background noise and any hissing sound that may emit from the microphone.

For external recording where a direct connection to a computer is not possible, the cheapest option is to use the video recording capabilities on your mobile phone. If you have an up to date model, the likelihood is that it will be able to record in full 1080p HD video or failing that, 720p. This is perfect for broadcasting on YouTube. The drawback with using a mobile phone to record your content is that it is not easy to connect an external mic so the sound quality will not be as crystal clear as it would be if you were using a dedicated mic. As long as the quality is legible and there are no high pitch sounds, viewers will be prepared to accept this as long as the content is immersive.

For more specialized videos, Warren suggests a DSLR camera. This kind of camera allows you to connect a microphone directly. If you have a high budget, you can simply buy external recorders, for example the Zoom H4N (cost you around $300.00) to adjust by hand and monitor the audio.

In similar fashion, lighting is important. You can perform your basic shooting in natural light, however halogen lights /reflectors would cost around $14.00-$20.00.

Finally, editing software and the computer are crucial. There is a one-click editing feature in YouTube. Macs and PCs have default editing programs for necessary editing. For high quality editing, you'll need a software called Adobe Premiere, Sony Vegas, or Final Cut X, depending on your resources and funds.

However, any recent Mac or PC laptop which has an Internet connection is sufficient for editing and uploading content to YouTube.

Video editing is what could ultimately make your broadcast stand out from the crowd. Even the most polished videos will contain issues where you have mispronounced a word or stuttered over a sentence. Rather than start the entire recording again from the beginning, these issues would be repeated in isolation, either at the time of mistake or after the full recording has been completed. They will then need to be knitted into to final production in a way that gives the viewer the perception that the video was "right first time".

The addition of graphics to your final presentation is also important as this will give your broadcast an identity. It is important that you keep the style of these graphics consistent from broadcast to broadcast as this will help your branding if a viewer can easily recognize your work, simply by seeing an image or a unique text and color style when they open up one of your broadcasts.

Once the production routine has been developed, you can experiment with style, different types of marketing and content. The benefit of having a newly made channel is to test what works well and what does not.

More tricks for Earning and Creating Traffic

Although we've covered a lot of good content and methods for creating income using YouTube, there are some other solutions you can use to create revenue through this platform. Rather than seeing YouTube itself as a way to monetize on its own, try to view it as a useful catalyst you can utilize. It's most valuable as a network, and not as the end product itself.

Alternative Earning Methods on YouTube:

- **Using Shopify:** We've already told you that YouTube is in second place for the place of the largest search engine on earth. When thinking of marketing, it would be foolish to ignore this huge resource you have available to you for free. But how can you take advantage of this? When it comes to physical products, Shopify is a good website to use for your e-commerce store, which you will then link to from YouTube.

- **Seeing Videos using Yondo:** When you have a goal of earning money from just your video content itself and not by using the videos to redirect people to buy physical products, there is a better choice than just hoping for high ad revenue. Make a channel, get a following, build your business brand, and then start directing your video audience to landing pages that will set them up with premium content and videos. One good way to do that is Yondo, which allows you to make a personal store for selling videos using your domain. This gives you the choice to sell monthly subscriptions and rentals that go on pay per view. But the best part is that you can set your own price and won't need to split your revenue with YouTube.

- **Using Sponsorships:** When you look at YouTube creators who are the most successful, you will soon see that there are sponsorships and ads on or in their videos. Typically, these represent opportunities the creators have found by themselves. The best thing about using these sponsorships is that the money you earn is all your own, and YouTube doesn't get a big cut of it. In addition to this, you will be able to negotiate the contracts that you wish to negotiate as needed according to your audience size. Usually, the number of revenue you get from these sponsorships adds up to more than you'd earn from just ad revenue.

Of course, this doesn't mean you shouldn't try to benefit from both! Then you will have a couple of different income streams from just one source, and what could be better than that?

- **Think about Live Speaking Eventually:** Another way to increase your reputation on YouTube is to attract engagements for live speaking to your channel. If the channel you are producing on YouTube has a specific audience or niche, conduct some online research about any conferences or events that are happening and need speakers. You can then use your statistics on YouTube, along with your top clips, then pitch yourself to the people directing the events in need of speakers. Being involved in these types of engagements is a great way to earn money. In fact, you can earn up to thousands with just a presentation lasting a single hour. Don't miss out on this chance and always look for different ways to make your audience grow.

Think Creatively to Earn a YouTube Income:

Are you able to earn real income using YouTube? Of course you are. Will you do this by only relying on ad revenue based on audience impressions? That isn't as likely. Rather, you should identify methods that you can use to leverage the gigantic network on YouTube to bring streams of revenue in and earn a massive passive income. You might try to do this and find that you aren't receiving as many likes, subscribers, or views as you want. That's because there is no shortage of competition on YouTube, with all of the creators and viewers on the site. You might now be asking how you can make your content gain exposure and stand out in the crowd. Here are some tips you can use to do that.

- **Do Video Transcriptions:** One way to make your videos more successful and attractive to viewers is to transcribe the content in the video and post it inside of the description of your video. Websites are not yet able to fetch keywords accurately from the audio spoken in video content, so at this time, written words are a big factor for the rankings of videos. If you already have a good presentation within your video, use speechpad.com or other similar resources to transcribe the words and get plenty of SEO boost for your ranks. Then paste this into the description field of your video. That makes your video simpler to absorb and consume and will lead to a boost in your rankings along the way.

- **Make a Video Reply:** YouTube lets you post comments as a video reply when it comes to some videos, meaning that videos you do publish allow others to leave you a response as a video comment. This will then reference your content and show underneath your video. This also works the opposite way, too. You can look up a video with a lot of views and leave your personal video as a comment response. This will lead millions to see your content, simply because you did this. But remember that this can only be done one time, so make your choice carefully and wisely. For example, if you are posting videos about apps for Android, find the most popular video about this and post yours as a video reply.

- **Make sure you Direct Links to your Content:** The majority of people view outside SEO as a method for boosting existing rankings for their personal domain pages. However, this also can matter a lot in your YouTube video's rankings. When you can get plenty of high sources or authority blogs to direct people to your videos, they will gain a higher keyword ranking and get more visitors. From your personal page, viewers will see more details on your video content which will then heighten the rankings there, too. This will eventually lead to a popular video network feeding huge amounts of traffic to each other and constantly getting bigger and bigger.

In order to save yourself some time working with external SEO, visit a site like AudienceBloom.com and use their service to your advantage. But there is another trick for this. When you use your blog to embed your video content, underneath the video you can add another link that leads back to the video. Make sure that you enter information about what the video is about here. This then improves the SEO juice your content has. The majority if videos on YouTube will not have other links pointing back to them, so this trick will help you go far.

- **Inserting other Videos:** Okay, so now you have put in a lot of hard work to get others to watch your content and videos. This is a great chance to show related content as the very end of your existing videos. If people have watched your video all the way to the end, this is the time when they are the most interested and engaged with it. If, with each video you create, you add links to your other content, you will have a big network of videos that interlink to each other, adding to your traffic and overall rankings. It would be a shame to miss out on this opportunity.

As you can see, there is a theme that recurs in these simple tips and tricks. They are easy and simple to apply to everything you create. What that means is that you are able to use this no matter what type of video you have to create more comments, subscribers, likes, and views overall. And since you are also linking to related videos, your empire of videos will grow and grow, leading to plenty of visitors and interested leads to your brand and site each day. This is how you earn money using YouTube.

YouTube Audience Growth Secrets 2019

Getting Traffic via Facebook

Go visit a fan page where your potential customers might be at.

Let's say your reviewing a shaving product, then you go find a big community where people are interested in shaving.

The first thing you need to do is create a conversation with other people.

Once you build that initial contact, you can start giving them suggestions on how to shave better, how to choose a shaving cream, how to choose an electric shaver etc.

You can then post your video url and make sure that you give them some valuable content.

Alternatively, you can also create a Facebook community for shavers. I recommend that you only do this once you got a few hundred views on your video because you want to confirm first if there is really a market for that product. By the way, it's totally up to you! Some of my students create their Facebook fan page first and it turned out profitable for them.

Tutorial Videos (How Tos) :

There was a 70% increase to these kinds of videos in 2017.

That implies that the number of views for these videos almost doubled in 2017,

then you can imagine how much we expect this to increase in 2019...

I am particularly a fan of these kinds of videos,

I mean why go through so much trouble reading an entire textbook on how to do something when you could learn it practically by watching someone else do it?

So, if you are very good at ding something, or you know how to do it, you can make *tutorial videos* about it on YouTube.

It's really simple to do this, you don't even have to be an expert at doing it, as long as you know it enough to teach it on YouTube, go for it! Whether it's Mathematics (a very budding niche on YouTube) or how to make beads or interior decoration, there is an infinite number of things people need help learning.

Even you can create other types of content like compilations.

Title and Thumbnail:

It doesn't matter how great your video quality is, if no one clicks on it, it's a waste.

It has been proven over time that thumbnails and titles are two major reasons people consider before they decide to watch a video from a channel they are not yet subscribed to.

The thumbnail gives a preview of your video, especially when someone else decides to embed your video on their site.

After choosing to use a custom thumbnail for your video you can upload a video thumbnail that you created. Here's how to do that:

> Go to the "Video Manager"
>
> Select the video you want to edit and click "edit"
>
> - Select "Custom Thumbnail"

Tips for choosing your thumbnail:

Ensure you have a human face on the thumbnail that expresses an emotional reaction to something.

Reactions like excitement, joy, sorrow or sadness, confusion, amazement, etc., shown on a thumbnail have been found according to scientific research to draw the attention of viewers.

All top YouTubers use it, even scammers use it to get views on their videos. I have fallen victim of it many times.

But the sad part is I had viewed their videos before I realized it was a scam. It helps if you are very attractive and even if you don't consider yourself that way *you can go on Pexels.com* to find lovely pictures you consider attractive and use them as part of your thumbnail...

Whatever you do however, ensure that the pictures are relevant to your video else you would be driving viewers away from your channel because they will consider you insincere and possessing no original content and would definitely not subscribe to your channel.

YOUR VIEWERS WANT TO SEE VALUE IN YOUR CHANNEL THAT IS WHAT WOULD DRIVE THEM TO SUBSCRIBE AND THEY WOULD BE STRONGLY REPELLED BY LIES.

The photo of a cute animal and that of a toddler have similar effect, however use only relevant photos.

Arrow and circles (one or both) on parts of the thumbnail draw viewers attention by creating curiosity about what they represent.

- Bright colors are very important. Black and white too can be used too because they would stand out of a stream of colorful thumbnails, so be dynamic.

The title however should be both very descriptive of the content of the video and attractive at the same time. Make your title descriptive enough to catch a viewer's attention and short enough for them to read at a glance.

Your title shouldn't be so lengthy that it would be cut off from the display, then you would be disadvantaged… You need to keep it short because your viewers want things QUICK and EASY. Everyone desires the magic pill, if you can portray this in your title, then you're good to go. Here are some tips that would help:

Try to use words in the superlative like, "top", "best", etc.,

You may capitalize key words but don't overuse them, they could be annoying to your viewers.

The use of the word "secret" stirs up curiosity and it has been proven scientifically to increase participation.

Starting titles with "Top X (an amount) …" boosts views.

The use of "Versus (vs)". For example, Samsung galaxy S8 vs iPhone X.

- Shorter time frames for great tasks. e.g. Build a professional website in FIVE minutes.

Although you should pay attention to the keywords I have mentioned above and use attractive adjectives, don't make it so "over the top" that it would look like clickbait. Take a second to look at your YouTube history, do you observe a pattern? Look at the titles of popular YouTubers, if you consider them clickbait level 10, then yours should be level 8. Level 0 is not enough and level 10 is too much. See this example

Level 8: Top 5 Mouthwatering Mexican Recipes That Blow Taco Bell Out Of The Water

Level 10: TOP 5 MEATY MEXICAN RECIPES 2019 BEST NEW RECIPES GONE WILD NSFW UNCENSORED

Use other *Social Media Platforms* to promote Your videos

This is one of the most effective ways to grow your YouTube viewers.

It is important to know that your prospective viewers do not belong to the YouTube social community alone.

They belong to other social communities like Facebook, Twitter, Instagram and the rest.

If you were to stick to YouTube for the promotion of your channel then you would be robbing yourself of many opportunities get viewers on your channel.

A cool step to take is *join a Facebook group related to your niche and post links to your videos there…*

One video at a time, do it slowly and respect the rules of the group. It is a great way to get a lot of subscribers on your channel: You could tweet big YouTubers and ask them for a shout out to promote your channel. It is important to make yourself valuable to these YouTubers as well and we would discuss some more about that soon.

YOU CAN CREATE A PROMOTIONAL FACEBOOK VIDEO AND LINK IT TO YOUR YOUTUBE VIDEO OR CHANNEL. Facebook prefers you use the Facebook live feature instead of sharing YouTube links.

Learn from your best performing videos:

Through Google Analytics you can find out your top performing videos. Take time to check what these videos have in common and what promotional methods you used for them and use them for your future videos.

Collaborating With Co-Youtubers To Promote *Your Channel*

Collaboration would boost your channel very fast especially if you do collaborate with channels that already have a large subscriber base!

It's like the same advertisement opportunities that accrue to product marketers who intend to promote sales for their products by *contacting a YouTuber with so many subscribers,* such an advert would reach more viewers because of the large subscriber base of the channel.

The same applies when you have a popular channel name you or refer people to your channel, you get more subscribers because of that. This was the purpose of YouTube descriptions in the past, but now there has been added a new YouTube collaborator feature…

With this feature you can ascribe credit to anyone who collaborates with you by entering their YouTube username and their channel's URL.

You can follow these steps for a successful collaboration to occur.

Check for compatibility: The success or failure of a collaboration is contingent on this factor.

You may not be able to successfully collaborate with a channel whose content is directly opposed to what your channel stands for or has nothing to do at all with what your channel represents. For example, you run a channel that is dedicate to makeups and you want to collaborate with a gaming channel or a cooking channel. In that case you would be said to be incompatible with that channel, except you find a way to *complement each other* which is possible at times. Compatibility isn't just limited to channel content but also personalities and character.

COME UP WITH AN IRRESISTIBLE IDEA: Ideas are foundational for a collaboration. **If you intend to collaborate with someone then you must come up with an idea for the collaboration.**

If you have no idea then you have no collaboration, else what do you intend to propose to the popular YouTuber that you collaborate in? Here's how to come up with your idea? The idea of collaboration is that you offer the YouTuber a collaborative idea that would benefit both of you.

Hardly would you find someone to promote you for free. This time you are not paying with money, you are paying with an idea.

The idea must be useful and beneficial to the person you intend to collaborate with, therefore, make it irresistible. The idea should also be something you would participate in and thus be given credit for by the collaborator, this is how you get more subscribers. At the end of it, both of you gain something. Your ideas must essentially be valuable to your collaborator such that it would get their attention and make them accept your offer. In your choice of a collaborator you should aim high but not too high.

As a small YouTuber, you could approach someone with ten times your subscribers.

- **Make an Offer**: Most collaborations involve a famous person collaborating with someone who is less famous. So, it is expected that you be the initiator of the collaboration. You have to make an offer first. You need to discuss how you intend to share the proceeds from the offer. All these plans must be concluded first in your planning and idea generation stage before you actually get to make the offer to our prospective collaborator, it indicates seriousness to your collaborator. You also need to make effort to promote the collaboration after the terms are settled, it secures people's attention to you even before the actual collaboration. You can do this by promoting your video on social media before it's release. After the release, you could use hashtags for promotion. With the hashtags you can link up many conversations on your video together. Most big brands use hashtags for the promotion, so why should you also? For instance, Heineken's hashtag is "openyourworld". In order to encourage your fans to use hashtags include them in the titles, your description, use them in the video and use them as YouTube card. The idea is to get your fans and your collaborator's talking about the hashtag thus encouraging more persons to view your videos.

Finding Collaborators

You could use any of these options to seek out collaborators for your video:

> YouTube Community Forum
>
> YouTube partners on Google+
>
> YTtalk forum
>
> YTgamers forum
>
> Tube buddy community

- *DamnLag*

You have a better chance at building a relationship with potential collaborators if you spend enough time making yourself known on these forums or on Skype. Better still, if you live close to a famous YouTuber and you have something cool that could help them, like a drone, there's your startup line for a relationship.

Consistency is of the essence when it comes to gaining and maintaining your subscribers and views on YouTube...This doesn't necessarily mean consistency of schedule, which creates anticipation among your viewers, but can also mean *consistency of themes, personality, format, or other things.* **These aspects keep people interested**. If you suddenly put up unrelated videos, then it will only confuse your subscribers.

If you wish to diversify your channel, then wait for some time.

Add in videos on new topics only if your subscribers have said ok to it.

You have to please them in order to hold on to them.

Collaborating with other YouTube creators is a great way to boost your fan base.

It not only makes the video that much **more awesome for the subscribers of both the channels**, but it also helps you brainstorm ideas in a better way and create higher quality stuff. *It's a win-win scenario* where your subscribers are introduced to the other person's audience, and their subscribers are introduced to yours.

You cannot collaborate with someone that has only a few viewers…

You would end up getting only a few from theirs, and all yours will subscribe to theirs, which is not fair.

You need someone who has at least as much as you or slightly more,

But if you think their work is under-appreciated and there is a lot of potential to increase your viewer base by a large margin, then you can go ahead and collaborate with them.

But remember, you have to work everything out before you collaborate in order to avoid any discrepancies.

Advertise to Make More Money

YouTube allows publishers to run advertisements on videos.

In exchange for this, YouTube gets a percentage of the revenue generated from these ads.

The YouTube Partner Program can be used to generate income through this method.

Some users believe that the publisher should revert to the program and start publishing ads a little while after starting their channel.

First, gain an audience and subscribers based on the **quality of content.**

THIS WILL KEEP THEM ON FOR THE LONG HAUL !

You can then put in ads without your viewers getting annoyed.

*They have higher chances of staying online and **watching the complete video including the ad.***

The Partner Program is usually available to those who have generated a specifically large number of views on their videos in a given amount of time.

I'm going to say this:

It is irrelevant to you whether the subscriber has bought anything from the advertiser or has watched the video fully or not.

ALL YOU CARE ABOUT IS PUTTING IN THE AD FIRST, **AND YOUR MONEY IS GENERATED**…

…You can tie up with as many companies as you like, and it will depend on how many videos you have to offer the public,

Signing up for these is fairly easy.

You just need to give some PayPal or bank account details for the transactions to take place.

Now,

YouTube is the second largest search engine online after Google.

30+ million user per day,

Everywhere we look, we see guys and girls, young and *old*, educated and dropouts,

who are sitting at home, filming videos and **making more money** than most lawyers, economists, and even CEOs.

Aren't you agree?

Their Secret?

THIS PEOPLE KNOW HOW TO BUILD A MASSIVE AUDIENCE!

If you don't like the idea to spend $1000 on a 26 weeks *outdated* Course...

Don't worry

I have you covered,

I'm going to teach you exactly How to Grow Your Channel/Business **organically in 2019**,

Cheap, without spend a lot of money

I suggest you check my new book **"Youtube Audience Growth Marketing Secrets 2019"** which is available on Amazon/Audible.

You will make more Leads, Sales & Profit today from your own subscribers:

Conclusion

Let's hope it was informative and able to provide you with all of the tools you need to achieve your goals of earning money using YouTube.

Since YouTube is the biggest video platform on the internet today, it would be a shame to waste the potential it provides you for earning a passive income.

The next step is to create engaging, quality content that focuses on being helpful and giving, getting a quality video setup, *and driving traffic to your YouTube page.*

This will then allow viewers to see a link to your store. You can also try asking for donations or using ads, as described in the book.

Made in the USA
Lexington, KY
02 June 2019